SEXING CHICKENS:

SEXING

CHICKENS

*AND OTHER STORIES SPUN FROM THE
OUTLANDISH HISTORY OF ENFIELD CT*

PETER FLOYD SORENSON

DEDICATION

This book is dedicated to the many people and establishments who populate the stories within this book as well as those who helped me uncover some of these tales which otherwise would have been relegated to the dustbin of history.

If I've forgotten or overlooked any individual contribution I apologize and will be sure to include you in the follow up book of additional stories – as there are too many untold tales left to tell.

A few individuals come to mind:

- Mike Miller
- Thomas Heath
- Dick Stevens
- Holly Samociuk
- Bill Friday
- Shari Jackson
- Andrew Francis Cote

AUTHOR'S NOTES

This book contains twelve rich tales about events or individuals unique to the town of Enfield and villages of Thompsonville, Scitico, and Hazardville, Connecticut.

Every time I meet another person in my adopted town I'm introduced to another story about another amazing resident, like when I met Holly Samociuk at the Wallop School (a one room schoolhouse owned and managed by the Enfield Historical Society) and she related a story about her uncle Thomas Ash Jr., a WWI army pilot.

Chance meeting, interesting tale.

For someone like me the Town of Enfield is a playground filled with endless stories to research and in which to immerse myself. The most interesting aspect to me in this process is that so many of the people in the town have never heard of some of these stories.

For instance, one of the tales in this book is centered around the 3500-seat outdoor boxing arena in Thompsonville where world champions fought as amateurs. It was erected in 1933 and existed until the mid-1950's – yet no one remembers it and I have yet to locate a single photo of the arena itself, even though the events played to a packed house. No promotional items like posters. No memorabilia kept by local promoters.

Difficult for me to believe that memories fade so quickly, yet it has afforded me the amazing opportunity to tell these stories again for the first time to a new readership, and I'm grateful for the chance to do so.

Some of these stories here are melancholy in nature, for example businesses that once flourished yet chose to leave for other pastures – either due to economics or poor decisions by well-intentioned politicians – which left a gaping hole in the community. Or the story herein of Paul Robeson who was initially welcomed with open arms by the townspeople and then, years later shown the door – a painful story that could have revealed the strong social and moral backbone of an immigrant community and ended up demonstrating just the opposite.

One tale reveals how an Elder Shaker, long dead, has revisited lands that he once walked and on which he toiled for an undetermined reason. Why do the deceased return? What might be their purpose?

My sincere hope is that you enjoy this collection, and, if you are a resident of Enfield, consider your lucky in calling this town your home. If you live outside this town, consider moving here, like I did just a few years ago.

Peter Sorenson
October 2023

Last note: Although the people, companies and events in this book are real, it may be that they are remembered and considered in a different light than they have been portrayed in this book by themselves and by others. No malice or bad intent is meant in how these individuals or companies have been represented within these pages.

TABLE OF CONTENTS

0: DOWN ON THE FARM

Sometimes buildings burn.

Sometimes by chance.

Sometimes on purpose.

Pyromania is a type of impulse control disorder characterized by an extreme attraction to starting fires, which, when successful, satisfies the individual's desire. It differs from arson as pyromania is not a conscious criminal act.

Arson is malicious and done with criminal intent, as we will see.

Pyromania, though intentional, is strictly pathological and compulsive.

Incredible as it may seem when one considers the concept of traditional incarceration, inmates at the Norris G. Osborn Prison Farm on Shaker Road in Enfield, Connecticut, were gifted the kind of liberties that convicts only 21 miles due south at the Wethersfield State Prison could only dream of at that time.

The prisoners at Osborn didn't wear state issued garb which might identify them as inmates during their period of containment. Those convicted of crimes were almost indistinguishable from the men assigned to guard them.

In fact, most prisoners were, at times, better armed than their overseers, such as during harvest time when inmates were issued razor sharp farm implements while the guards carried nothing to protect themselves or to enforce their authority.

At best the situation made for an uneasy détente.

On July 15th, 1947, prison guards Harry F. Wallace and William M. Jones were sentenced to six months imprisonment for the crime of smuggling alcohol into the Osborn Prison Farm, where it was then distributed amongst the inmates. Harold E. Helm, a former guard at the facility, was given a suspended sentence and one year's probation for the same crime.

In addition to delivering spirits, Jones, a blacksmith at the site, had acted as a courier, carrying mail in and out of the institution. As payment for this service Jones was provided with coal, food, and other state purchased goods for his personal use by "inmates with connections".

Wallace had begun his illegal activities innocently enough while accompanying two inmates on a delivery of farm produce, specifically potatoes, to a customer in Southbury, Connecticut. On the first leg of the fateful trip with one of the inmates behind the wheel, as was often the case, the trio stopped to purchase liquor at a package store. It is unclear if Wallace put up any resistance or was a willing accomplice.

On the return leg of the trip the group made three more

stops for more liquor, as Wallace had seemingly given his tacit approval to the purchases.

From that moment forward it was easy to blackmail the prison guard into making frequent deliveries of spirits to the penitentiary.

Harold E. Helm's engagement exposed the power and authority given to the inmates, which some willingly abused. Bert Nearing, a convict assigned to the superintendent's office at the Prison Farm oversaw the scheduling of hours and work duties for the prison personnel. In exchange for deliveries of liquor, Nearing, the convict, gifted Helms, the guard, holidays like Christmas off to spend with his family.

Before Wallace, Jones, and Helm were sentenced, the States Attorney General Meade Alcorn, who was prosecuting the case against the former employees, took the institution itself to task:

> *The prisoners are granted astounding liberties. There are no bars, no gates, no weapons in sight, only a fence surrounding a group of buildings. The very system provides a background of opportunity…"* [1]

He continued:

> *"So long as the legislature sees fit to send men there who are supposed to be receiving penalties, we must guard against a recurrence of this.*
>
> *At the prison in Wethersfield the discipline is severe."* [2]

Alcorn laid the blame for the guard's actions not on the sentries themselves but on the institution, as if the prison

---

[1] Prison Farm System Hit and Defended. (1947, July 16). The Hartford Courant. Page One.

[2] ibid

had been on trial, and the accused unable to morally function within the prison walls.

In passing sentence Superior Court Judge Ernest A. Inglis countered Alcorn's opinion.

"While it may be a fact that the system at the farm was lax, it may also be true that the system is considered good penology." [3]

At its core it hadn't been the system that had been at fault but the guards who had broken trust with the system.

Walter Borys was born to Polish immigrant parents Walter and Catherine in 1917. Like many in their community the elder Borys worked along with four of their children at the Thompsonville Carpet Factory and made their home in the same section of greater Enfield.

Young Walter, tagged with the name 'Tricky' in high school, elected a different career path from his parents and siblings, being employed as a guard at the Osborn Prison Farm located at the former Shaker Village.

Four months after the trial of the three Osborne guards, on a cool crisp Friday afternoon, guard Walter Borys, known for his acute awareness and knack for being at the right place at the right time, noticed flames erupting from the hayloft of a renovated Shaker barn while on patrol. The building was one of three interconnected massive structures measuring 40 feet wide by 100 feet long. The fabrications were used to store produce and grains harvested on the farm for use not only at the prison but at other state institutions, as well as to sell for a profit to subsidize prison operations.

Stockpiled within the walls of the framed edifices on that

_____

[3] ibid

day were:

- 300 tons of hay
- 60 tons of grain
- 600 tons of silage
- 500 bushels of potatoes
- 400 bushels of beets and
- lesser quantities of other vegetables

Borys quickly sounded the alarm to which both guards and inmates alike responded. As the fire leapt from one building to the next the responders released the herd of 192 cattle into the prison fields.

Fire Razes Three Barns At Osborn Prison Farm

Loss Put at $100,000; Inmates Lauded for Saving Cattle; Hay, Grain, Vegetables Destroyed

Thompsonville, Nov. 11—In the most destructive fire which has occurred in Enfield in many years, three huge connecting barns on the Osborn prison farm in the east part of the town were destroyed by fire this afternoon. $100,000 Loss

The three buildings, each a two-story construction, one with basement, were approximately 100 by 40 feet in size, and the loss on the buildings and their contents is estimated by the superintendent, George H. Bradley, at approximately $100,000. Destroyed with the buildings were 300 tons of hay, 60 tons of grain and 600 tons of ensilage.

Continued on Page 9

The six-alarm fire was raging as firefighters and equipment arrived from Thompsonville, North Thompsonville, Hazardville, East Longmeadow (MA), and Bradley Field, a regional airport which had only opened six years earlier as an Army airbase. Firehoses drew a steady supply of water from the canals which ran throughout the property, having previously been constructed by the Shaker sect, the religious group which had vacated the site years prior.

By late that Friday evening, through the collective efforts of the firefighters and the inmates, as well as due to the dwindling supply of consumables, the flames were brought under control. A decision was made to leave the Bradley chemical pump truck on site overnight to address any flareups that might occur.

The loss of buildings and goods was estimated at $100,000 (or 1.3MM in 2020 dollars), a substantial loss.

An investigation of the fire began once conditions allowed. Lieutenant Frank Starkel and officer Frank Whelan reviewed the scene for the State Fire Marshalls office, although their credentials and expertise for doing so remain unclear. Deputy Warden Burton J. Caswell of the Wethersfield State Prison carried out an independent investigation of the fire. Likewise, how being the second in command of a state penitentiary prepared him for the task is suspect.

The initial finding of the independent investigations into the fire was that it was of a benign origin.

Eleven months later Arthur Martin, Osborn parolee, was arrested by the state police and charged with arson for the same Norris G. Osborn Prison Farm fire.

Whoops.

The arrest wasn't due to the investigative work of state employees but because that old saying rings true - *there is no honor among thieves.*

In an act of self-preservation, John Valentino, a former Osborn inmate who had been incarcerated during the same period as Arthur Martin, turned in his former cellmate for his role in starting the prison conflagration of 1947.

Valentino, a convicted burglar and counterfeiter, had found himself in a bind when authorities picked him up in New York on a parole violation. Recognizing an opportunity, he offered up Martin.

HELD IN BONDS, RESULT OF FIRE AT PRISON FARM

Arthur Martin, Parolee, Accused by Another Inmate of Burning Barn

Thompsonville, Nov. 4—Judge Arthur R. Roelick in Enfield Count

Working with the Connecticut State Police, Valentino encouraged Arthur Martin to reminisce about the event in Room 303 at the Palace Hotel in Waterbury as the conversation was recorded. Martin confirmed he had started the fire in the Osborn hayloft by inserting a lit cigarette into a book of matches, dropping the assemblage, and leaving the scene, which had provided him with enough time to establish an alibi.

Twelve months after his arrest and arraignment, and at the conclusion of a short three-day trial, Arthur Martin, former Osborn farm inmate, was sentenced to seven to thirty years to be served at the Wethersfield State Prison on a charge of arson - malicious and done with criminal intent.

Martin would experience the type of justice espoused by the Connecticut States Attorney General Meade Alcorn.

Swift and stern.

Norris Galpin Osborn was born to (father) Minot Augur Osborn and (mother) Katherine Sophia (Gilbert) Osborn on April 17,1858. He was the last of nine, and one of only six that lived past birth. The Osborn family could trace their lineage directly back to colonial settlers, and through them to members of the English aristocracy.

The Osborn family made their home in the sixth district in New Haven, with Norris attending Hopkins Grammar School, one of the oldest preparatory schools in the United States.

The Hopkins school had been established in 1660 by Edward Hopkins, the second governor of the Connecticut Colony who had set up a trust to fund the institution. The school's stated purpose was to the "breeding up of hopeful youths...for the public service of the country in future times." [4]

The school encouraged good works, focusing on molding men of character. Corporal punishment was rare and "employed only for the most serious of infractions like repeated misdemeanors, escaping the premise while under sentence, or for addressing the school with an obscene epithet." [5]

It was in those hallowed halls of fine education, where Norris's sense of right and wrong was formed, as well as his

---

[4] Mission & History | Hopkins School, n.d.

[5] ibid

understanding of how punishment should fit a crime.

After completing his studies at Hopkins, Osborn entered Yale College, as was befitting a young man of his stature. Upon graduation with a Master of Arts degree, he worked at the New Haven Register as a reporter, the then-respected newspaper being owned by his father and edited by his brother-in-law.

Within four years Norris had succeeded his relative, twenty years his senior, as editor of the venerable publication. During that period Osborn had wed Katherine Louise Gardner, and the couple had settled down in the city of his birth and had begun growing their family.

Osborn took no time in establishing himself as a man of values, morality, and character. It was written about him, after his passing in 1932:

> *"His knowledge of the practicalities of life enabled him to be a great service to the college and the city of New Haven in many of the natural conflicts which arose between the men of the town and the men of the gown."* [6]

In addition to his duties as newspaper editor, Norris was appointed as a member of the State Prison Board in 1895 and became known as a student of prison reform. Once again, after his death, the Hartford Courant noted:

> *"He had a wide range of sympathies and an intimate understanding of human nature which amounted to genius."* [7]

By 1912, after seventeen years on the committee,

---

[6] Col. Osborn, Editor, Dies At Age Of 74 (May, 7 1932) *Hartford Courant.*
[7] ibid

Osborn was elected president of the State Prison Board. Years later, reflecting on the man, the President of Yale College James Rowland Angell noted:

> *"He will always be gratefully remembered for his devotion to the public welfare, for his indomitable courage, and for his trenchant and relentless attacks on whatever he saw evil."* [8]

Norris Osborn had received his military title of "Colonel", not because of military service, but due to his appointment as a respected member on Connecticut Governor Thomas H. Waller's staff. It was a common practice to add a military title to laymen as a sign of respect.

Colonel Osborn considered his appointment and membership on the State Prison Board as a calling and spent countless hours getting to know a great many inmates in the state's penal institutions and what reformations might address their struggles.

One example is the charge he led in 1923 to encourage the legislature to repeal the *Whipping Act*:

> *"It is part of the general practice of penitentiaries to resort to whipping in addition to the penalty of imprisonment, where a convict proves idle or insubordinate. The warden of the State's prison of Connecticut, under the General Statutes, in case any prisoners ', are disobedient or disorderly, or do not faithfully perform their task, may put fetters and shackles on them, and moderately whip them, not exceeding ten stripes for any one offence, or confine them in dark and solitary cells.'"* [9]

---

[8] Ibid

[9] WHIPPING AND CASTRATION AS PUNISHMENTS FOR CRIME (June 1899) Yale Law Journal (vol VIII no 9)

Osborn had succeeded in moving women to their own prison facilities (1918 Connecticut State Farm and Reformatory for Women) and removed the criminally insane from the general prison populace to a new institution in Newtown, Connecticut (1929 Fairfield State Hospital).

By 1930 the Colonel had convinced the state legislature of the need for a new minimum-security prison for men. That same year the state purchased a sixteen-hundred-acre tract of land in Enfield, Connecticut, formerly known as the Shaker Farm. Once renovations on the site were completed it was opened as a new penal institution.

For the better part of the first year the new facility

remained unnamed and was simply referred to as the Prison Farm. But after the revered New Haven editor passed away on May 4, 1932, at the age of 74, the State Prison Board passed a resolution christening the penitentiary the Norris G. Osborn Prison Farm to honor the man and recognize his efforts in ensuring the humane treatment of lesser criminals.

After the death of Colonel Norris Osborn, the northern region of Enfield seesawed between the promises and the challenges of the prison farm.

Like many penitentiaries at the time, inmates became unpaid employees producing all types of products which were then sold to help offset the cost of internment.

In 1933 a proposal was put before the legislature to refocus activities away from manufacturing shirts to educating prisoners. The movement to do so was a direct result of the passage of the Hawes-Cooper Act of 1929, which was set to go into effect on January 1, 1934. The act gave the right to individual states to prohibit the import and sale of inmate produced goods manufactured in another state.

In 1929 the nation had been ravaged by the financial impact of the collapse of Wall Street which had begun on October 24, of that year known today as Black Thursday, and manufacturers, employers, employees, and labor leaders had agreed that they could not compete with *the free labor force* provided by penal institutions.

The first phase of the Franklin Delano Roosevelt New Deal had just begun in 1933, and its impact would not be felt for years. Commerce was in full protection mode and prison manufacturing was an easy target.

Connecticut was not alone in producing goods with prison labor, nationwide 52% of the inmates at 104 prisons were involved in some form of manufacturing, with 60% of finished products exported for sale to other states.[10] Most of the profits from good sold were used to buffer the cost of incarceration.

Penal institutions were not alone in pushing back against the legislation. The American Prison Association opposed the Hawes-Cooper Act, but not due to the financial impact aspects but on how it would sideline worker inmates which would result in an idle population. Against still opposition the act was eventually upheld by the Supreme Court, which stated that American manpower could not compete fairly with convict labor.

Idle hands would now be the Devil's workshop.

Even with activities to fill their days, the desire to be free compelled enough inmates to escape the Osborn Farm with disconcerting regularity.

William H. Clark escaped the minimum-security prison on August 12, 1935, and was believed to be at large in Massachusetts when the following opinion was published in the August 22nd edition of the Thompsonville Press:

Not the Type Promised

It is not surprising that some of the residents of the east part of the town are becoming nervous over the "breaks" at the Osborn Prison Farm. Some of them in fact, especially following the recent escape, have become jittery over the situation.

When the state authorities decided to experiment with

---

[10] Hawes-Cooper Act. *Encyclopedia.com*

a prison farm in this locality there was naturally some objection. This, however, was waived aside with the assurance that the type of prisoner that would be confined would be harmless.

They would be men whose conduct has given positive assurance that they will not be guilty of the slightest untoward action, we were told. 'Men', said the late lamented Col. Norris G. Osborn in discussing the matter here with a group of citizens, 'whom you would admit into your own home.'

But they have turned out, in some instances at least, to be no such type as described by the genial Colonel in selling the idea to the community.

The last prisoner [Clark] to make his getaway particularly fails to come up to these specifications. One wonders how many more such types are to be found among the approximately 200 confined at this farm at the present time.

One wonders, too, if the prison authorities are exactly keeping faith with the people of this community and especially the neighborhood that is affected by this situation. It is thought that the last thing that the type of prisoner to be kept at the farm would think of would be to escape, but apparently this is not so in every instance.

The knowledge of this fact is not adding much to the comfort or the peace of mind of the residents in the prison farm area. This is not at all surprising for an escaping criminal is the last person most of us would want to meet up with at any hour of the day or night. It would seem as though the authorities should be more circumspect in the character of the prisoners sent to the

farm and select them more in keeping with their
promises when the farm was established here.

Hardly the type one would, in the words of Colonel Osborn, *invite into your home*, recent prison farm escapee William H. Clark, also known as William H. Frost, William H. Nelson, Willian Ryan, and Henry Teed, was added to the Justice Department's list of public enemies by order of J. Edgar Hoover on November 6, 1935.

William Clark would remain at-large for ten months.

Clark could hardly be considered a conventional minimum-security class prisoner as he had been previously interred at Wethersfield State Prison in Connecticut, Sing Sing Prison in New York, and Charlestown State Prison in Massachusetts. Neither was he the type of convict that one would expect to land on the Public Enemies list as he had been a career burglar, a "break and enter" specialist.

And at sixty years old he hardly seemed capable of inciting fear in the general populace.

He was finally captured in New York by prison parole officer George H. Bradley.

In an uncommon display of understanding, Clark, who could have been charged under the habitual criminal statute which carried a maximum sentence of thirty-nine years, was charged instead with the simple crime of escaping prison by State's Attorney General Hugh H. Alcorn.

Maybe Alcorn was getting soft, or perhaps he was just tired from having to re-charge Osborn escapees.

Over the next few years Prison Farm fugitives exposed a downward trend in the type of prisoner housed at the Osborn Farm. The following, with their year of escape followed by their particulars, are examples:

- 1938 – Carl Phillips serving a seven-to-ten-year

sentence for burglary with violence

- 1938 – Edward Winski and Donald Simpson serving twelve-to-twenty for armed holdup
- 1939 – Charles H. Wilson serving one-to-three for arson
- 1939 – James Childs three-to-five for manslaughter
- 1940 – Fred Stearns three-to-five for raping his eighteen-year-old daughter
- 1940 – Wayne Swanson three-to-seven for aggravated assault with intent to rape

In 1940, as Stearns and Swanson roamed free, the town was gripped in a collective fervor over the threats posed by escaped inmates from the Norris G. Osborn Prison Farm.

It was best summarized by an open front-page letter to Connecticut Governor Raymond E. Baldwin printed in the August 8, 1940, edition of the Thompsonville Press:

An Open Letter

TO GOV. RAYMOND E. BALDWIN

Dear Governor:

Escapees from the prison Farm are becoming so regular as to constitute a huge joke, That, however, is a problem of penology.

Escapees, however, are affected with a distinct public interest here, when those who escape are the type of prisoner who should never be on a Prison Farm.

So far as we can determine the Prison Farm must be a favorite place for sending sex criminals. The Prison Board might consider how women of this town feel when such a prisoner escapes.

A Prison Farm should never house a violator of women, or a subverter of the morals of his own daughter.

The whole business is disgraceful. Sometimes we think some branches of the public service are blind to seeing, and deaf to hearing, when complaints are made.

These escapees with attendant public fright here have been called to the attention of Prison authorities. The answer has been profound silence. These escapees are matters of public knowledge throughout the entire state – but, it is our womenfolk who suffer from fright and fear when these things happen.

The horrible murder of Miss Lodi, perpetrated in Springfield yesterday, could have been the murder of a local woman. It could have been a more severe crime, the type known as sexual murder, differing from the Lodi case.

The people of Enfield are entitled to look to their State Government for protection, and particularly, to protest against such errors of judgement in penology, as to permit prisoners convicted of sexual crimes to roam with comparative freedom.

Ten years ago, the late Colonel Norris Osborn came here and publicly promised that no violent prisoner would be incarcerated here at the Prison Farm. That promise has been broken. The State of Connecticut has broken Faith with the people of this community.

It is up to you Governor. Our frightened and enraged citizenry demand a reform covering all phases of this horrible mess. What do you propose to do about it?

Just the day before, on August 7th, 1940, one of the escapees referred to in the letter, Fred Stearns, had been recaptured in South Windsor and taken to the State Penitentiary in Wethersfield.

He had not been returned to the Osborn Farm as the authorities considered the potential fallout and public recoil.

During their period of escape the body of Rose Lodi, only twenty-two years old, had been found slashed to death and sexually compromised in the bushes of an area called the *hobo jungle* of nearby Springfield, Massachusetts. Based on the timing of their escape and the deviant nature of their past crimes both Stearns and Swanson were immediate suspects.

Although Stearns was quickly cleared of suspicion, the uneasy relationship between the town and the penitentiary had been publicly laid bare. And Swanson had yet to be recaptured.

The escapes were the 12th and the 13th of the short ten-year lifespan of the prison. Even after the capture of Stearns the local police continued to field calls from anxious area women who had heard noises in their cellars or had seem people of suspect character in their neighborhood.

It was clearly a town on the edge.

Five months later Robert Powers, also known as Robert Peters, who had been convicted of attacking his estranged wife with a knife, escaped the Osborn Prison Farm.

Powers had made a career of crime, having initially been arrested as a youth of 14 for breaking and entering in Bridgeport, Connecticut. From there he had continued to run askance of the law, either serving time for various crimes or having sentences suspended for reasons unknown. At 30 years of age the habitual offender represented the most recent concern for an already anxious town.

Wayne Swanson, sex offender, was still at large adding to the unease of the community.

Escapes continued with at least one recorded per year.

Perhaps it was time for a more unusual event.

The sightings referred to as the Washington Flap, the Washington National Airport Sightings, or the Invasion of Washington, took place over a period from July 12th to the 29th. The event captured the entire nation's attention as a series of unidentified flying object sightings occurred at our nation's capital, with the most serious taking place on two consecutive weekends of July 19-20 and 26-27.

The military and the government did their best to explain away the events, but numerous outlets had reported on the swarms and the people's attention had been captured.

Two months later, on September 5th of 1952, Walter L. Rochette, pilot relations manager at the Trumbull, Connecticut, airport, contacted the Air Force and Navy Chiefs of Staff requesting that they transmit a message using the most effective radio communications to the flying saucers observing the planet that they were welcome to land at the regional airport.[11]

Included in the message were the geographical coordinates, landing conditions, and dimensions of the

---

[11] Trumbull Airport May Become First Saucermen's Field. (September 5, 1952), Hartford Courant, p. 36.

airfield landing site. Rochette's request concluded that:

> *"...it is important to the mental wellbeing of this planet that your existence be verified and that your intentions be classified as friendly."* [12]

The Ground Observer Corps (GOC) was first instituted to help protect the United States against an air attack from a foreign enemy during World War Two. Civilians were tasked with the job of scanning the skies and reporting anomalies to their local *filter stations* which would investigate and forward authenticated reports to the Aircraft Warning Service (AWS).

Although the original GOC program had been retired in 1944, a second iteration was launched in 1950 as a direct result from the chill of the Cold War.

In 1952 the new GOC program was expanded to include new volunteers ranging from seven to eighty-six years old and was referred to as Operation Skywatch. The volunteers numbered 750,000 working in shifts at over 16,000 posts and 73 filter centers.

One of these *filter stations* was in New Haven, Connecticut, and was commanded by Major Richard J. Curtis, who was scheduled to retire at the end of September of 1952.

As they say, "timing is everything".

On September 6th, at 10:10 in the morning, only one day after Walter Rochette had requested the Air Force and Navy transmit his request to the *beings in the heavens*, Walter Borys, on early guard duty at the Osborne Prison Farm, heard and

---

[12] ibid

observed a strange event in the morning sky. At that moment both he and fellow guard George McCracken, better known as 'Jeep' to his friends, a nickname acquired and recorded in the high school publication the Enfield Echo, were in charge of a thirteen-inmate detail on the prison grounds.

Borys stood transfixed as a silvery oblong object, not unlike a dinnerplate, emitted a sound unlike any jet or airplane as it hung high above in the northern sky.

Without warning the sound stopped and the craft began to drift toward the ground in a zigzag motion. After what seemed a considerable drop the object erupted with a loud report, a puff of smoke, and shot up at a right angle at an incredible speed.

You could hear the proverbial pin drop.

After a moment the guard realized he wasn't the only one staring at the diminishing point in the sky. The thirteen inmates under his watch had simply stopped in midmotion and stood slack jawed. Turning he caught McCracken's gaze, gathered himself and reported the incident to Francis D. McCue, acting captain of the guards, who, in turn, notified Osborn Farm Superintendent George H. Bradley.

Word spread quickly and soon area Civil Defense officials William J. Murphy and Russell Maylott arrived at the site to interview each witness in turn.

Except for minor discrepancies all fifteen recollections were consistent.

Although the incident was reported to the Filter Station in New Haven no official record appears in Air Force files.

One can only believe that perhaps Walter Rochette's request had been received and had been responded to by the saucermen circling the planet.

Twelve days later Audrey H. Hennis posted a short opinion in the Hartford Courant claiming the object was unequivocally a jet.

Her credentials and expertise on the subject are suspect.

By early the following year events returned to a more sublime nature, with the 130th annual banquet for the Enfield Society for the Detection of Thieves and Robbers held on the grounds of the Osborn Prison Farm. President of the organization, Edgar H. Parkman would welcome Nathaniel Leverone, Director of the Chicago Crime Commission, as the speaker for the event.

Normalized by this time, 1954 welcomed yet another inmate escape, this time by James Dixon who was serving a two-to-eight-year sentence for indecent assault. Assisting in the capture of the fugitive was a helicopter on loan from the Kaman Aircraft Corporation of Bloomfield, Connecticut.

1955 saw another annual Thieves and Robbers event take place at the Osborn Prison Farm. This time the topic was of more of a local interest as a new state prison was being proposed to be constructed east of the existing Osborn facility.

Almost difficult to believe was that prison inmates served as waitstaff at the event, moving freely among the two hundred and seventy-five participants as sharp cutlery adorned each place setting and the opportunity for mayhem presented itself openly.

Like Groundhog Day, another Osborn inmate, Raymond Burkett, serving a two-to-ten-year sentence for indecent assault, escaped the prison confines in 1956. Once again helicopters were pressed into service, as well as bloodhounds, to track the prisoner. Inconceivable to most with even relatively little intelligence, Burkett had but one year left to serve at the minimum-security institution when he made his break. His capture resulted in ten years being added to his sentence.

1957 challenged the conventional view of the concept of the *dangerous inmate* as the state offered twelve Osborn prisoners the opportunity to participate in a new forestry program. Men were provided the tools necessary to clear trees including chainsaws and axes while the officers guarding them remained unarmed. Understandably the inmates had been thoroughly screened for their engagement and were also aware of the weight of the responsibility accorded to them to ensure the program was a success.

Certainly, Norris Osborn would have been delighted.

But incarcerated men are, at their core, designed to run counter to expectations, and so during the second year of the forestry experiment, Arthur Davies, serving a two-to-five-year term on seven counts of breaking and entering, broke as well from a Stafford, Connecticut, conservation camp where he had been working clearing trees.

Considering the average IQ of chronic offenders is 15 points or more below that of most adults[13], Davies was, not surprisingly, recaptured.

After all it was winter when he had made his escape.

It had snowed the previous evening.

The guards simply followed his tracks to find him.

As 1960 approached the end of the Prison Farm experiment was in sight

---

[13] Ellis and Anthony, Crime, Delinquency and Intelligence (2003) pp 343-365.

By 1959 the first section of the new State Prison in Enfield had been completed and fifty inmates from Osborn had been transferred to the facility. Not surprisingly these were the very men who had been scrutinized and selected for the forestry detail. They had already been identified as less problematic than their peers.

For the state the timing couldn't have been better as many of the buildings at the Prison Farm, constructed during the Shaker period, were considered unsafe and potential firetraps.

In a nod to the *lax security* label ascribed to the Osborn Prison Farm years before, the new facility was double-fenced, with an inner fence twenty-feet high and an outer of ten feet. The perimeter was lit at night and monitored from seven towers equidistantly spaced around the site.

Honoring the approach established at the beginning of the farm, inmates would continue to be treated humanely with an eye toward reducing recidivism. After all, as Mark Richmond, warden at the Wethersfield State Prison had commented years earlier:

"...brutality begets brutality."

In 1960 the Enfield Correctional Institution was completed, replacing the minimum-security Osborn Prison facility, and received its first inmates in 1962.

A maximum-security facility was constructed on the same property in 1963, and another minimum-security institution was completed in 1985.

The original penitentiary was referred to as the Osborn Prison Farm until 1986 when it was modified as a medium-security facility. The remaining dairy operation had been shut down in 1977 when the herd of 400 dairy cows had been auctioned off, and the equipment dismantled or sold.

Several hundred acres of prime farmland were still being planted and harvested in 1985, producing some 700 tons of hay and 2,000 tons of corn silage which were sold to area farmers.

As of this writing Connecticut prison populations are decreasing, and the penal institutions on the old Shaker property are in the process of closing operations.

Soon there will be nothing left but memories.

1: WHAT'S SHAKING

It's an unassuming house on the banks of Shaker Pond, or Shaker Pines Lake as it is now referred to by the Association managing the bedroom community.

Built in 1900, the four-bedroom, two-bath home, with a two-car detached garage and water access comes complete with its own resident spirit.

Yes – a Shaker *spirit*.

Without attempting to retell the story of the Enfield Shakers it's enough to know that the religious community was established in 1792 on land donated by David Meacham.[14] The Connecticut enclave grew to a total of five families, the North Family, South Family, East Family, West Family, and – at the center – the Church Family occupying nearly 3,000 acres of prime croplands.

Assigned the name Shakers for their penchant for physically gyrating when the spirit of the Lord overtook them, the "Shaking Quakers" were known for their superior

---

[14] Clark, B. Stories Carved in Stone. p 192.

livestock, fine orchards, culinary arts and recipes, seed business, and fine craftsmanship.

Well, that and their penchant for speaking with those who had passed over.

Many find it surprising that the Shakers were avid Spiritualists and believed it was possible to converse with the dead. They had been receiving messages from the spirit world since the earliest days of their history, but an internal religious revival in the 1830s and 40s, called the Era of Manifestations, combined with the growing popularity of Spiritualism among the public around the same time frame, brought an increase in spiritual activities and messages from the beyond.

> *"Some mediums [are] at the Church Family from New York. We [will] go down this afternoon to a séance held in Church's meeting room."*[15]

The Elder and Eldress leaders were appointed by the Church Family ministry, while other roles were appointed by the Elders and Eldresses of each family. At its peak in 1855, the Enfield Shaker community had between 35 and 40 members per family. The Elders/Eldresses were responsible for the spiritual and physical well-being of their family, while the deacons/deaconesses were responsible for the family's domestic needs. Trustees were responsible for all business transactions with the outside world.

The Enfield Shakers created Trip Hammer Pond, now referred to as Crescent Lake, which borders Enfield and East Longmeadow, Massachusetts, as well as Shaker Pond, now referred to as Shaker Pines Lake by damming each

---

[15] "Beautiful and Important Wonders": The Shakers and Spiritualism. Shaker Heritage Society of Albany New York. This entry was recorded in the Shaker Church Family Journal on September 8, 1889.

body of water. The ponds generated power for various mills, which included:

> ...*three sawmills, three cider mills, a carding machine, a pail factory, plus a trip hammer and lead pipe plant.*[16]

The lead manufactory was erected at the end of Trip Hammer Pond, thusly named for the type of machinery used for the shaping of the lead pipe.

At the sawmills on Shaker Pines Lake the men would spend their time:

> ...*roughing out lumber for future needs, or perhaps a day at the lathe in the workshop turning pegs or chair legs or whatever was needed to complete [their] project.*[17]

As local historian Mike Miller noted in a web article:

> *The Shaker movement lost momentum in the 1850s and began a slow decline as American society evolved. Industrialization—and the opportunities it created—opened new options that were more appealing than the celibate and strictly controlled Shaker lifestyle.*

> *People—young men in particular—ceased to join in any numbers. Most children raised by the Shakers left when they reached the age of choice.*

> *In Enfield, the West Family closed in 1854 and the East Family in 1874. Membership in the remaining families continued to dwindle, and those remaining had to rely increasingly on hired help to operate the*

---

[16] Challenge Of Change. pg 172.
[17] IBID pg 41

farms.[18]

Jean Paul Cote was one such hired hand.

Jean Paul Cote [Paul Cote], emigrated into the United States in 1880 from La Belle Provence [Quebec], Canada. Born in 1852, he was married to his wife Emma, two years his junior. Cote was employed as a farmhand by the Shaker community, as the local sect needed experienced help in working on the farmland. By all accounts the young man was a competent and valued employee.

Accustomed to the harsh Canadian winters Cote didn't give the inclement morning weather of Sunday, March 11, 1888, a second thought as he went about his chores, after all, as the saying went, March comes in like a lion and goes out like a lamb.

This day, though, would bring the full force of the lion.

A day that began cloudy and rainy soon turned colder, with the precipitation changing to hail, sleet, and then snow.

Lots of snow.

A classic nor'easter.

As the day progressed the winds picked up, soon reaching a steady 40 miles per hour, with gusts to 60.

By midday the weather prompted the Shakers and their workers to bring the cattle and other livestock into the barns as a precaution. Cote was instructed by his employers to head home to be with his wife as the region was in the grips of a full-fledged blizzard.

Bundled up against the storm, Cote mounted his horse and headed into the breech, but soon found himself in a whiteout, snow-blind, unable to determine where he was or how to get home.

---

[18] Miller. Enfield's Shaker Legacy

He realized without a miracle he might die.

Being a man of quick wits with the kind of savvy reserved for Canadian farmhands, Cote dismounted and reaching up, found the steeds mane, ran his hand to the haunches and grasped the horse's tail.

With a few words he urged the mare to go home.

And slowly, methodically, the beast calmly navigated the winter maelstrom, leading himself and Cote safely back to their Thompsonville residence, five miles away. The beast safely bedded; Cote sought refuge in the warm embrace of his wife. [19]

Was his survival a Shaker miracle or simply due to common horse sense?

View of North Main Street Thompsonville, 1888. (EHS Collection)

As the Shaker families grew smaller, others saw

---

[19] Interview with Andrew Francis Cote. February 19, 2023.

opportunities. One of these individuals was 31-year-old Frank Swetland [Sweatland] of Shaker Station [Enfield] who rented Shaker Pond and adjacent grounds to:

> *Erect a large pavilion for dancing and swings and will charge parties a small fee for the use of the grounds and boats, As Mr. Swetland is a Christian gentleman his object in securing control of the premises is to prevent desecration and make the place so respectable that the best people of this and the adjoining states will consider themselves honored by patronizing it.[20]*

On the west bank of Shaker Pond, the entrepreneur cleared out undergrowth and, as promised, constructed a large pavilion and cookhouse, installed see-saws and swing sets, and erected a candy and confectionary store. As noted in the Thompsonville Press in their August 1908 edition:

> *The success of the undertaking was soon assured, and Pine Point Grove, as Mr. Sweatland [sic Swetland] called his resort, soon became a popular place for all first-class parties. Encouraged by the support accorded, rowboats were placed upon the lake, and later a steamer was added. The resort was conducted upon very strict principles, no Sunday pleasure seekers nor Sunday selling was permitted. Parties from miles around enjoyed the pleasures afforded at Pine Point.*

Swetland tired of the venture in early 1899 and sold his interest in Pine Point to Wilbur F. Duncan of Warehouse Point, a village in East Windsor.

Duncan was a regional real estate mogul of the period having bought and sold numerous properties during the late

---

[20] The Hartford Courant. May 30, 1882 edition. News of the State. pg 4

1880s and early 1890s. In 1908 Duncan was party to the largest land deal the town of Manchester would experience for years. In the winter of 1907 Wilbur Duncan and Edward Lockwood purchased a 50-acre tract of land in the city, subdivided the property into 218 building lots and sold the site to Lee, Bright, & Loring, a land development firm from Boston[21].

Duncan knew how to spot opportunities and how to profit from his acquisitions.

Pine Point Grove represented such an opportunity.

By May of 1899, only a few months after acquiring the Shaker Pond property, Duncan applied for a license to sell ale, lager beer, Rhine wine, and cider at the Pine Point Grove facility. It represented a drastic change in direction from the reverent approach that had been established by Swetland years before[22].

Three months later, in August of 1899, Duncan turned around and sold the site to a group of Hartford investors whose reported interest was in establishing both a trolley line to the grove as well as constructing a "Summer Hotel" along the lakeside[23]. Included in the sale was a 20-year lease of Shaker's Pond, with a privilege to renew.

Duncan was not only the "seller" but also a member of the purchasing investment group along with Thomas Perkins, Leslie Newberry, Wilbur E. Goodwin (a West Hartford Selectman) [24], and Frederick C. Rockwell.

---

[21] Hartford Courant. July 25, 1908. pg 14.

[22] Thompsonville Press. June 15 1899 edition.

[23] Thompsonville Press. August 17 1899 edition.

[24] Hall, William H. The History of West Hartford. 1930. pg 55.

The Courant reported the intentions of the Hartford group as to their proposing of a new route of access to the property to the state.

> *W. E. Goodwin, F. C. Rockwell, W. F. Duncan, Thomas C. Perkins, and Leslie W. Newberry have expressed their intention to apply for a charter for a road to carry freight and passengers. It is proposed to begin this road at a point at the intersection of the state line between Massachusetts and Connecticut and the main highway from Enfield to Longmeadow, thence over private lands to what is known as Brainard Road, to Shaker Station in Enfield, through Pine Point Grove and to any points on Shaker Pond that may be deemed for the best accommodation of the public. These petitioners ask for permission to buy and hold pleasure grounds along the line of the railway.* [25]

Prior to the charter submission the property was transferred to the New England Construction Company (NECC) which had been capitalized in 1897 with the goal of:

> *…building and equipping street railroads [trolleys], electric light plants, water works, gas works, pipelines in this and other states and to buy, sell, and pledge bonds, stock, and other properties of other companies acquired in the course of business of this company.* [26]

One of the stockholders in *NECC* was ex-Governor Thomas M. Waller of New London, Connecticut.

Here is where the interrelationships of the various parties and ownership becomes somewhat convoluted.

---

[25] Hartford Courant. December 9, 1900 edition. pg 8.
[26] Hartford Courant. July 22, 1897 edition. pg 11.

Frank Swetland circa 1882. (member photo Ancestry.com)

Prior to the involvement of NECC, Wilber E. Goodwin, a member of the Hartford investment group, secured a $2000 loan against the *Pine Point Grove* property [$72,000 in 2020], the money being obtained from a state school fund. From the records available it seems as if it represented a new mortgage on the property, which would indicate that ownership of the location was never conveyed to NECC. Perhaps NECC was involved in securing Goodwin's loan as facilitation was also part of the services their firm provided.

The primary interest of NECC was in the potential of building the railway to the Pine Point Grove site, as that was the focus of their business. It's safe to assume that rather than site ownership it's more likely that the construction company was engaged in the Pine Point Grove venture in a partnership of sorts, with the expectation that the General Assembly would approve of the proposed trolley line to Shaker Pond.

To further muddy the waters, in early September of 1900, Duncan transferred his Pine Point Grove liquor license to Emile A. Grise, who was at the time the proprietor of the Hazardville Hotel, indicating a possible change in ownership as Grise was identified as owner/manager in the June 27, 1901, edition of the Thompsonville Press:

> *E. A. Grise,* **proprietor** *of Pine Point Grove, announces as attractions at the grove July 4 a single scull race, a bicycle race in Marth Hubbard costume, a cake walk, and dancing afternoon and evening. A shore dinner will be served.*

At this point in time Pine Point Grove either had three owners, or some type of ownership or management arrangement between some or all of them. Slightly confusing at best.

Regardless of ownership, activities were moving forward with respect to the hoped for trolley line to Shaker Pond. The formal public notice of the intention of the group to submit their petition to the Connecticut General Assembly in January of the following year was published in the December 18th, 1900, edition of the Hartford Courant[27].

By January 11th the group had filed their petition for the trolley plan with the state. One of the investment group members, Wilbur E. Goodwin, filed an additional petition requesting the incorporation in the state of the Pine Point Tramway Company[28] while a fellow member filed a petition for the incorporation of the West End Railway Company in the towns of Hartford and West Hartford. [29]

Hopes were high and those involved waited for the approval of the state.

Instead, disappointment was delivered.

As reported in the Hartford Courant, even as six other proposals were passed by the state Senate:

No Pine Point Tramway

The Senate, upon the motion of Senator Burton, receded and concurred with the House in rejecting the resolution incorporating the Pine Point Tramway Company.

The petition for trolley access was once again voted down in June of 1901 as part of another amendment:

… not to revive the rights of the Enfield & Longmeadow trolley road to build a branch to Shaker Pond in Enfield.

---

[27] Hartford Courant. December 18, 1900 edition. pg 8.
[28] Naugatuck Daily News. January 11, 1901 edition. pg 2
[29] IBID

This action seemed to be the death knell for the idea of constructing a Summer Hotel on the banks of Shaker Pond, and quite likely led to the waning interest of the Hartford Investment Group in furthering their consideration of developing the site as well as removing the possibility of constructing the line for the New England Construction Company.

To add insult to injury Clarence B. Force of Farmington filed a suit against Fred C. Rockwell and Wilbur E. Goodwin, investment group members, for non-payment of surveying work he had performed on the Pine Point tract targeted for the trolley line. [30]

Two Thompsonville Press articles in 1904 and 1908 referenced the struggles of the site in the early 1900s.

The resort afterwards declined in popular favor, owing to the way in which it was conducted, as its new owners were less careful as to the parties which they allowed to picnic there, and the place soon lost its good reputation.

The lack of patronage resulted in the owners giving up their supervision of the place, the pavilion and cook room were allowed to stand year after year without repairs, and the boats and the steamer were left in the water during the winter season with the result that what were not stolen went to pieces or were sunk. [31]

The owners had not only lost interest after the failure of the trolley initiative, but it also seemed as if neither the mortgage nor the taxes had been addressed leading to:

Foreclosure proceedings have now been commenced, and at a hearing in the superior court in Hartford last Friday Attorney General William A. King appeared

---

[30] Thompsonville Press. February 21, 1901 edition. pg 3
[31] Thompsonville Press. August 6th, 1906 edition.

for the state, and it was shown that neither interest nor taxes have been paid in several years, the interest due amounting to $465.02, a total of $2,465.02 aside from taxes and costs.

The property consists of 100 acres of land, a pavilion, a storehouse, icehouse, and some sheds. Besides the natural deterioration, forest fires have swept over part of the property, and its present valuation, as estimated by deputy Sheriff Wilson and Charles Brainard, summoned as witnesses, was from $800 to $1,000.[32]

How far the vision of Frank Swetland had fallen.

On June 8, 1905, a white knight of sorts appeared as Amos D. Bridge acquired the Pine Point Grove site for less than the outstanding mortgage in a foreclosure purchase.

In a celebratory mood, on January 21, 1906, Bridge threw a party for the 130 men in his employ at the Hazardville Institute Hall. In a bit of irony, Emile A. Grise, former proprietor of Pine Point Grove and owner of the Hazardville Hotel across the street from that evening's venue, provided and served the dinner.

Interesting bedfellows.

Unfortunately, Amos Bridge, the former Senator, would die from heart failure nine months later and would never see his vision for Pine Point Grove manifest.

His interest in the Pine Point site lived on through his sons, as by July of 1906 they had begun to clear the site, rebuild and renovate pavilions, and had installed six new rowboats on the pond. A new cottage had been constructed on the water's edge, which was available to rent, foreshadowing its future development.

---

[32] IBID

By 1913, through further land acquisitions, the Amos D. Bridge's Sons Company controlled a contiguous tract of land that was 6 miles long and two miles wide on the west side of the Hartford & Springfield branch of the New York, New Haven, and Hartford Railroad stretching from Hazardville to East Longmeadow Massachusetts. Included in the acreage was the Pine Pont Grove property, which was now a settlement of a dozen rentable summer cottages[33].

1913 proved to be a year of change as, after 141 years of peaceful existence, most of the Shakers left the town of Enfield moving to either Watervliet or Lebanon, New York, or West Pittsfield, Massachusetts.

The North Family closed its doors in 1913, leaving only a handful of Shakers occupying some of the Church and South Family buildings.[34]

One of the last acts as the group exited, was to sell Edward W. Walsh and George B. Robinson of East Longmeadow, Massachusetts, Trip Hammer Pond and about one hundred acres of land extending up to their hometown.

Much like Bridge's Sons had done on Shaker Pond, the duo planned a summer cottage colony of over 500 individual lots around the pond. A quick renaming of the water followed, as Crescent Lake sounded much more attractive to potential purchasers than Trip Hammer Pond. Crescent Park lots quickly sold to businessmen, professionals, and others from Springfield and East Longmeadow, Massachusetts.

A final sale of Shaker land to private investors occurred the following year.

On November 24, 1914, the Shaker property was

---

[33] Hartford Courant. July 28, 1913. Page 11.
[34] Miller. Enfield's Shaker Legacy

> *sold to John B. Stewart of Windsor, Connecticut, and John Philips of Wendham, Massachusetts. The sale agreement allowed the Shakers to remain on the property for the rest of their lives, but the last three left Enfield in 1917 for other communities.[35]*

Like the sale of the other properties, Stewart and Philips had formed a stock company which purchased the 1600-acre tract. The new syndicate, of which both men were board members, was formed with the stated intent of developing real estate and carrying on a general farming business[36]. According to the Norwich Bulletin the new company would concentrate on farming tobacco,[37] a more regionally representational pursuit and certainly more reflective of how the Shakers had managed the acreage.

In 1927 General Electric introduced the first household electric refrigerator, costing about $500 [$7,000 in 2020]. Up until that point families relied on the "icebox", originally created by Thomas Moore, a farmer and cabinetmaker from Philadelphia, Pennsylvania.[38]

Ice would be harvested from ponds and lakes in the winter and stored for use throughout the balance of the year in large local or regional storehouses. It would be delivered via horse-drawn carriage to homes, usually daily, in blocks of between 25 to 100 pounds.

Just like it had been done in other industries where controlling the market helped support artificial prices and ensure profits, ice was no exception. "Ice Trusts", groupings of select companies who mined, stored, and sold

---

[35] IBID

[36] Stafford Springs Press. November 25, 1914, edition. pg 2.

[37] Norwich Bulletin. November 24, 1914, edition. pg 2.

[38] From ice harvesting to Icebox. (2022)

blocks of ice, were set up to control regional markets. Although the New York City Ice Trust may have been the more well-known, the Ice Trust of Hartford owned licenses to cut, extract, and deliver ice all over the state, marginalizing competition while maximizing profits.

Both Shaker Pond and Triphammer Pond were two of the finest ice fields in the state of Connecticut, with eighty acres of water producing crystal clear ice during the frigid New England winter months.

In October of 1904 the Shakers had signed a 20-year lease agreement with the Hartford and Spring Brook Ice companies, the Trout Brook Ice Company, and the Consolidated Ice Company of Springfield, Massachusetts to mine ice on both bodies of water. As part of the Triphammer Pond arrangement the Shakers reserved the right to cut 200 to 300 tons of ice from one edge of the pond for their own use.

The Shakers had expected the Ice Trust lessees, as part of the Triphammer agreement as well as based on the economical ice harvesting price, to improve the location to facilitate ice removal and storage, but as of 1906 no improvements had been made.

In fact, the lessees, members of the Hartford Ice Trust, had extracted no ice from either Pond at all in 1906, helping to limit the amount of marketable ice and stabilize pricing. The trust had maintained that the ice, at least in 1906, was not of sufficient thickness, but this was contradicted by the Shakers themselves, as they had harvested blocks of between six to eight inches deep from Triphammer Pond during late winter of that year. [39]

The Hartford Courant had reported that because the Trust had allowed 30,000 tons of ice to "rot away" there might be an indictment of the companies to follow. Not

---

[39] Hartford Courant, May 25, 1906, edition. page 1.

only had the Trust shirked their duty in harvesting ice, but they also had, for a profit, shipped large quantities of ice to other states instead of filling their own ice houses.

As a regional monopoly, the Hartford Ice trust had reduced, though buyouts, acquisitions, or forced closures, the number of competitors from 13 in 1905 to three in 1906.

Certainly, one would believe that the Shakers would never have supported the unethical practices of those with which they had signed an agreement. Then again, the ice revenues from the pond amounted to $200 per year [$4,000 in 2020] per pond, certainly nothing to be discounted, even when considered against the questionable actions of the Trust.

By 1915, against all odds, the Hartford Ice Trust was still "in business", despite the Sherman Antitrust Act of 1890, the Clayton Antitrust Act of 1914, and the Federal Trade Commission Act of 1914, each of which should have impacted the actions of the Ice Trust. But only the Sherman Act carried criminal penalties, which rendered the other acts impotent, so it was business as usual in the capital city.

In Enfield though, trouble was brewing.

George W. Clark, Miriam Offord, Joseph Holden, Catherine M. Allen, and Sarah Burger, all Shakers who previously lived in Enfield but had relocated to Lebanon, New York, filed a lawsuit in April of 1915 against Edward W. Walsh and George B. Robinson of East Longmeadow, who had purchased the Triphammer Pond property in 1913.

The plaintiffs had been Elders and Eldresses of the Enfield community and had been tasked as trustees and agents for the community.

Elder Walter Shepherd and Eldress Catherine Tate had originally deeded 100 acres of land to Walsh and Robinson including the waters of Triphammer Pond.

The problem was who had the rights to the ice.

Without the rights to the pond itself the Shakers had no legal standing to lease the pond for ice-cutting purposes. When the property had been sold to Robinson and Walsh there had still been 10 years remaining on the original ice harvesting lease the Shakers had signed with the Hartford Ice Trust, and, even if the Trust had neglected to mine the ice, the contract fees were still due.

The plaintiffs argued in the suit that Shepherd and Tate had lacked the authority to make the sale of the pond and property, as neither George Clark nor Miriam Offord had signed off on the sale, and the sale should be voided. [40]

Justice moves slowly, and before a judgement could be rendered in the case Elder George W. Clark passed away at 76 years of age, from

...an illness incident to old age. [41]

As a trustee, Clark would never experience the rightful reassignment of the water rights to the Shakers, waters which had provided ice to the community during the winter months and provided power to the mills constructed on the ponds all year round.

Finally, three years later, in 1918, the Shaker suit was

---

[40] Hartford Courant. November 13, 1915 edition. pg 5
[41] Berkshire Evening eagle. October 15, 1914 edition. pg 2

settled – out of court.

The basis of the settlement is that the boundary [of the property as sold] will be changed, as the Shakers claimed it should be, and the rights in the pond, instead of being possessed by Robinson and Walsh, will go to subsequent grantees of Shakers in another lot of land. The Shakers will receive part of the money that had been received for rental of the pond and held by the trustee [court appointed] pending the determination of the suit. [42]

And so, control of the waters of Triphammer Pond had been transferred back to the original owners and wrested away from the men from East Longmeadow.

The question remains though; for how long?

Cottages were being constructed along the shores of Triphammer Pond [Crescent Lake] and the pond was being used recreationally by new residents.

Did the reconveyance of the waters to the Shakers infer that control of the pond was limited to the harvesting of ice? Not if the boundaries of the sale had been truly redrawn to exclude the waters from the 1914 sale to Robinson and Walsh.

The new boundaries ceded ownership of Triphammer Pond to the people who had originally created the body of water – the Shakers. But with the Shakers having totally removed themselves from Enfield the year before the suit was settled in 1918, who would caretake the waters of Triphammer and Shaker Ponds?

---

[42] Hartford Courant. June 26, 1918 edition. pg 5.

Who would watch over them?

Perhaps the answer is found at Pine Point.

I was sleeping one night and was awakened by a voice from a man who must have been standing next to my bed and clearly wanted my attention.

I sat up.

There was no one in the room.

About thirty days later the entire sequence of events repeated itself.

Shaken, I mentioned the events to my daughter who responded "Yeah. They did the same thing to me, but they didn't come into my room." [43]

A few months later a 17-year-old sitter, hired to watch over the homeowner's daughter, was sitting in the family's living room, her back to the pond. At approximately 9:00 in the evening the temperature in the room shifted, growing noticeably colder.

The sitter looked up from her homework and an approximately six-foot-tall male in a hat and long coat stepped out of the homeowner's bedroom. The sitter was frozen, terrified, unsure of what she was witnessing.

His features were not crystal clear, but there was a recognizable shape to his face and his countenance was calm and not fear inducing.

The man stood there, watching, either looking at the sitter or perhaps past her to the waters that lay beyond

---

[43] 2023 interview with Shari Jackson of Shaker Pines Resort.

for what seemed like a long time to the young lady, long enough to be unsettling. The apparition did not respond when she spoke. Soon the figure disappeared.[44]

Elder George W. Clark (Enfield Historical Society archives)

---

[44] 2023 interview with Ellie of Shaker Pines Resort.

Weeks later a similar event occurred, but this time it was witnessed by the same sitter and the daughter of the homeowner.

> *Through the doorframe of my mother's bedroom I saw a man move inside, pacing from one side of the room to the other.*
>
> *The family dog stood in the hallway, looking in the same direction, his tail was wagging.* [45]

The owner, obviously concerned about the identity of the spirit personality, began to investigate who or what the apparition might be.

Knowing Shaker Pines [Shaker Pond] was previously associated with the Shakers sect, the homeowner picked up Michael Millers "Enfield" book, leafed through it and was immediately drawn to the photo of Elder George W. Clark, so much so she snapped a photo of it on her phone and sent it to her babysitter.

She immediately responded "That's him. Oh my God."

But why would George Clark choose this place to make himself known? What would draw the former Shaker to this home? Why would he feel at ease here, enough to manifest and even communicate?

Perhaps because the homeowner, like the Shaker, is a Spiritualist herself, a kindred spirit. If Clark had chosen to watch over the waters, then from what better spot than where the energies resonated with his own?

Much like Clark himself had written years before in the Shaker publication *The Manifest*:

---

[45] 2023 interview with Isabelle Jackson of Shaker Pines Resort.

From the land of the Leal they come, the silent visitors, more often unseen than seen, unfelt than felt, though occasionally the veil is lifted, and we see behind it, and we catch a glimpse of this wonderful world and its inhabitants.

Suddenly, while thus ruminating, a spirit form appeared but a few feet distant, revealing distinctly the head and face of a Shaker sister. The figure wore one of our ordinary bonnets. We eagerly scanned the features to ascertain if it were some[one] we had known in earth life but not being able to recognize her we asked -

"What was her mission?" [46]

And so, this gentle homeowner at Shaker Pines Lake might ask the same question of the visiting spirit George W. Clark, as the seasons pass and the opaque winter ice on the pond turns to a shimmering transparency in summer.

What is your mission?

---

[46] *The Manifesto* volume XXVIII. Angel Visitation. Shaker Publication. Pg 4.

2: SCITICO GOLD

Magical Thinking.

When we are young, we consider Santa Claus, the Easter Bunny, and the Tooth Fairy as real. We simply don't question their existence.

As we mature, we move past these characters, realizing belief in them requires a suspension of critical thinking.

Some might say that any religion requires the same level of suspension, and that we simply *allow ourselves to believe* based on nothing but faith, as if the commitment to our belief is validation enough.

The following is a historical story based in part on faith and a man's commitment to his beliefs.

In December of 1492, during his first voyage to the New World, Christopher Columbus happened upon an island in the Caribbean shaped like a turtle.[47] He named it, appropriately, Isla Tortuga.

---

[47] "Ile de la tortue, Histoire." Villa Camp Mandingue, Haiti.

Originally settled by Spanish colonists, the island was inhabited at different times by the Spanish, French, English, and Dutch from 1630 through 1670.

During that period independent French, English, and Dutch pirates, as well as contracted privateers, settled on the land and launched raids from its shores, mainly targeting Spanish ships.

One of these Dutch privateers was a buccaneer named Captain David Marteen whose greatest success, according to legend, was capturing the Spanish ship the Galleon Neptune in 1665, looting the ship and absconding with two chests full of Spanish minted gold coins worth 20 million dollars.[48]

To escape the wrath of Spain, who had sent ships in hot pursuit of the pirated treasure, the captain and crew sailed up the East Coast of America, entered Long Island Sound, then headed north up the Connecticut River at Old Saybrook.

Oft repeated stories hold that Marteen then sailed up the Farmington River, where it branches off the Connecticut River at Windsor, making landfall and setting up camp somewhere along the way. Versions further say that the group was attacked by locals and driven either upstream to the Salmon Brook River, where they buried their gold, or back to the Connecticut River to seek shelter elsewhere.

If the second possibility were true then logic would dictate that the band would not have headed south down the Connecticut River toward the pursuing Spaniards but would have continued north, possibly seeking shelter within the next navigable river - the Scantic.

It's the second option where this story draws local interest and suggests possibilities.

---

[48] www.treasureNet.com [Marteen various posts]

On March 31, 1848, Kate and Margaret Fox, of Hydesville, New York, reportedly contacted the spirit of a murdered peddler whose body had been found in the house. The spirit was said to have communicated through rapping noises which had been heard, at the time, by more than the two sisters, adding a certain credibility to the event.

The women became an overnight sensation, spawning the religious movement known as Spiritualism that maintained that a person's awareness persisted after death and may be communicated with by the living. [49]

As part of a greater movement American Spiritualists would meet in private homes for séances, at halls for trance lectures, at state or national conventions, and at summer camps attended by thousands.[50] Even Mary Todd Lincoln, in an attempt to emotionally recover from the loss of her son, organized séances in the White House attended by her husband, President Abraham Lincoln.

Surprisingly no spirit from the 'other side' communicated with American Spiritualists more frequently than the ghost of Benjamin Franklin. Spiritualist Josiah Brigham reported on the use of a heavenly machine, operated by the departed Franklin, to pass on inspirations and thoughts to mortals from the beyond.

In her treatise on Spiritualism, Ann Braude discussed the difficulty in relating to the quasi-religion for both the professional and the layman.

Spiritualism can be as problematic for the modern scholar as it was to nineteenth-century churchmen.

---

[49] Melton, Encyclopedia of Occultism & Parapsychology, p 1463
[50] Weisberg. Talking to the Dead

While it is ubiquitous in the documents of nineteenth-century culture, its adherents' abhorrence of organization makes their movement difficult to chart in retrospect. Spiritualists were united only by their attempt to make contact with the spirits of the dead. Many pursued this common goal in isolation from other believers, through distinctive means accompanied by distinctive ideologies. Some espoused Christianity, some condemned it. Some placed faith in messages delivered through mediums that their co-religionists dismissed as frauds.

The movement had no identifiable membership because it had no formal associations for believers to join. It had no official leaders because it had no offices for them to hold and no hierarchies to sanction them. It had no creed, no authoritative text.

Spiritualist luminaries set forth visions of ultimate reality so unique that many had to invent new words to describe the universe as they saw it. [51]

Somers, Connecticut, and to some extent the surrounding towns, was a hotbed of Spiritualist activity for most of the nineteenth century, and Somers's resident Calvin Hall was a regionally famed Spiritualist medium. His performances were regularly documented in local and national publications. A letter published in Volume 7 of *The Spiritual Telegraph* published in 1855 follows:

CURES BY SPIRITS

Milford, Ct., the. 19th, 1864

---

[51] Braude. P. 399

Dear Bro. Brittan:

Since I last wrote you, we have had a visit from some healing mediums, and although this is perhaps the very stronghold of Sectarianism, they have caused considerable investigation, and have been visited by some who would not have been expected out of the pale of church proscription.

The mediums referred to are a Captain Calvin Hall, of Somers, Ct., and a Mrs. Dexter, of Ware, Mass.

They came to Milford by direction, and found the place better prepared for sowing the Truth at the time than at any other since I have been acquainted here, on account of the supposed death and burial of a girl whom many believed to have only been in a trance state, and that she was buried alive. But even with this operating upon them, the people were so sensuous and superstitious they were refused a hearing on their first visit, but they have since visited here once a week, and have had a large number of calls for this place.

Captain Hall has certificates from various sources, of cases he has cured by the aid of the Spirits.

His treatment consists in making passes at the Spirits direct and giving only magnetized water.

Those treated in town have experienced much benefit.

Of his certificates I have taken off a synopsis, which, with the above, are at your service.

Dolly Hale, of Barre, aged 27 years, who had suffered extremely for three years from neuralgia, which had induced fits, after exhausting the usual sources of medical aid in Barre and Worcester, was directed by a clairvoyant to Captain Hall, and was cured in three weeks at his residence.

Mrs. Adeline K. Fletcher, aged 47 years, had the nerve of the right eye paralyzed for three years, and had nearly become blind in it, when sight was restored through the mediumship of Captain Hall.

Mary A. Francis, of Stafford, was relieved of a severe cough, after raising blood, becoming greatly emaciated, and having the lower limbs swell badly, by the manipulations. She had been a long time under the effect of anodynes to suppress the cough and took none after the operations were commenced.

Caroline Sibley, of Ware, was cured of a severe headache which had existed for about three months, and had resisted all remedies which she had applied, by Captain Hall laying his hand on her head and making a few passes.

Mary Adams, of Somersville, testifies that she had been in ill health for thirty years with what the doctors called 'liver complaint,' that her diet had been reduced by their order to one cracker a day with brandy and sugar, that she had a bad cough, had taken medicine for nearly 20 years steady, and had had fits from January to April, averaging three per week. Captain Hall cured her immediately of fits, her cough was relieved, and she commenced improving without the aid of drugs, or the use of tea, coffee, or spirituous liquors.

Sophronia Davis, of Somers, had been under usual treatment for a severe pain in her head two weeks, and had nearly lost her hearing, when on calling on Captain Hall, the pain was removed by his treatment and her hearing restored.

Lydia W. Gates, of Somersville, was cured of rheumatism and other difficulties.

Nathan Burlingame, of the same place, certifies that his wife was cured of severe dysentery by the operations—' the disease abating from that time. Under the peculiar influence the dysentery was cured.'

Peter Deming, of Somers, had his eye badly injured while cutting timber, by a bough springing and striking the sight, so that there was a scratch across it, and the ' eye looked more like blood than anything else and was very painful,' was cured by the operations of Captain Hall. 'The eye was almost immediately restored to its former color, and in a very short time was as free from pain as ever, and he could read a newspaper with as much ease as ever.'

Another case, where the patient was examined at a distance of miles from his bedside, and the disease was accurately told as decided by a post-mortem examination, was also certified. In this instance the diagnosis and prognosis differed from seven physicians who made the examination, and found the Spirits correct.

Yours, P. D. [52]

In the September 13, 1856, edition of *The New England Spiritualist* periodical Captain Hall was mentioned in a published letter and two announcements:

The first demonstration witnessed was at Brother Chauncey Barnes', in the village of Fair Haven, in

---

[52] The Spiritual Telegraph. p. 265

November 1854.

At this time, I met Brother Calvin Hall, of Somers; Mrs. Dexter, and Brother Fairfield, of Mass.; and they, together with Bro. Barnes and wife, laid their hands on the top of a very heavy piano, which very soon vibrated, rising up some two or three inches and again coming down to the floor. This was repeated several times, and then the piano rolled out on its castors into the middle of the room.

Though I suppose such now might be a very common manifestation, at that time, and to me as a skeptic, it was beyond comprehension. To account for the destruction of the laws of gravity, and the action of unseen power sufficient to raise such a ponderous weight, was a puzzle to the mind.

Bro. Fairfield was entranced and gave a communication purporting to come from the spirit of Emanuel Swedenborg, criticizing his own writings, a volume of which lay on a table in the room. He said they contained a good many truths; also, many errors, as his experience in the spirit world had well convinced him.

After some personations through Mrs. Dexter, the evening closed without my being able to detect any deception on the part of the mediums, who gave me the fullest opportunity to investigate that my mind could desire [53].

---

[53] New England Spiritualist. P. 3

New-England Spiritualist was a Journal of the Methods and Philosophy of Spirit-Manifestation, and its Uses to Mankind. Published from 1855 to 1858.

The paper included an upcoming list of the medium's performances:

Calvin Hall will be in Westfield, Mass., Mondays and Tuesdays; Chicopee Falls, Wednesdays and Thursdays; Springfield, Fridays and Saturdays, for four weeks from the 18th of August. [54]

In 1861 Hall erected a church in Somers, which he deeded, along with the associated horse sheds and land upon which they were constructed, to the Somers Association of Spiritualists.[55]

On Hall's passing, the Association refocused its activities to Somersville, Connecticut, 2 miles east of Scitico and 2 miles west of Somers. There they purchased four and a half acres with money Hall had left the group [in his will], unsuccessfully contested by other heirs. They then moved the Somers church to the purchased Somersville property on School Street, which they called the Spiritualist Hall.

The hall was used for numerous social activities beyond religious gatherings until 1917, when the Attorney General leveraged a 1905 law to wrest control over the property from the Spiritualists. In truth, at the time, the Association had only one living member, and he was living in an insane asylum in Massachusetts, so taking the property away was a relatively simple affair. [56] In 1933 Spiritualist Hall was razed in conjunction with other buildings to make way for Somersville Elementary School. [57]

But in the mid-to-late 1800's the area was enraptured with the concept of Spiritualism. Even the Shakers of Enfield were associated with the practice as noted:

Their beliefs were based upon spiritualism and included the notion that they received messages from the spirit of

---

[54] IBID

[55] Morning Journal Courier, June 22, 1880. P. 2.

[56] Biennial Report of the Attorney-General. (1919). p 25.

[57] United States Department of the Interior National Park, Service National Register of Historic Places section 8 p. 3.

God which were expressed during religious revivals.

They also experienced what they interpreted as messages from God during silent meditations and became known as "Shaking Quakers" because of the ecstatic nature of their worship services. [58]

With the prospect of communications from beyond an accepted possibility, it was not a surprise when an announcement was printed in the Hartford Times (reprinted in numerous publications including Scientific American) with a straight-line connection to the beyond:

The Latest Pirate Treasure Delusion.

A correspondent of the Hartford Times, writing from Hazardville, Conn., Jan. 1st, says that great excitement exists among the Spiritualists in Scitico and Hazardville.

One of the greatest spirit developments of the age, they believe, is about to occur, revealing to mortal man the hidden wealth and treasure which for three centuries has quietly rested in the earth, on the premises of Mr. Thomas Barrett, in the village of Scitico.

The circumstances are as follows : A. D. Putnam [sic A. W. Putnam], a lineal descendant of the revolutionary hero, who says he has recently been sent here from the State of California, through the influence of the spirit of Benjamin Franklin, has over-vigorously set to work three sets of men, night and day, paying at the rate of $3 per day, in digging a subterranean passage, which he claims to lead to a cave under a large hill, which hill is close to the bank of the Scantic river, a little west of the Scitico stockinet

---

[58] Stortz

factory, where the spirit of Benjamin Franklin assures him he will find valuables in the shape of diamonds and bars of gold to the amount of five millions of dollars, (!) which was deposited by Spanish pirates three centuries ago, who, after being hotly pursued, burned their ships at or near the mouth of the Connecticut river, taking their small boats and coming up the Connecticut, being closely followed.

They took the Scantic as far as Scitico Falls, calculating on taking an overland route to Massachusetts Bay, but being attacked by the Indians, and two of their number being killed, they deposited their booty in what was called a natural cave at that time, covering the mouth of the cave with stones.

Mr. Putnam says he shall enter the cave, if filled with wolves, angels, or devils; and if he is as successful in dragging from this subterranean vault the five million as his great-grandfather was in unearthing a she-wolf, clairvoyant mediums will be above par in this place.

There are a large number of persons visiting the spot daily, from far and near. Strangers, and those coming from a distance, will be furnished with a guide by calling at the shoe store of Mr. Thomas Barrett, the owner of the land.

The disposition to be made of the gold is as follows: Mr. Barrett, the owner of the land, has one fifth; the Governor of the State, one fifth, to be used for educational purposes; a gentleman in Boston, one fifth, to be used for the Catholic Society, as the Spaniards were Catholics; one fifth to the Spiritualists, and one fifth to Mr. Putnam. [59]

Interestingly the story held a direct connection to the fable of Marteen's buried treasure and to the possibility that he had buried his ill-gotten gold in Scitico of all places.

There were, of course, some discrepancies in the tale as the medium directing the search had claimed gold had been buried three centuries prior, when Marteen had visited only two centuries before. But a later article corrected the first insofar as Putnam's name A. W. (not A. D.), as well as adjusting the timeframe when the treasure was buried – two hundred years before, not three hundred, which would have fit Marteen's timeframe perfectly.

Reports of the Scitico venture were reported all over the country from New England to California and even overseas. Most of these were not firsthand accounts but re-reports captured from wire services facilitated by the introduction of the telegraph in the mid 1800's. Some added their own opinions or skepticism, as in the Massachusetts Spy article published on January 17, 1868:

> *The treasure which the diggers on the bank of the Scantic River supposed to be buried [sic] there, is $5,000,000 in diamonds and bars of gold, deposited by Spanish pirates 300 years ago. The pirates are said to have been pursued and burning their ships near the mouth of the Connecticut River, to have come in boats to Scantic, to hide their booty.*
>
> *As this is a clairvoyant story, it is advisable to get less excited about it than the diggers are.*

The January 18 edition of the Columbian Register

---

[59] Scientifc American. p. 49

published in New Haven, Connecticut, was more balanced:

> *Two Californians have appeared in Scitico, claiming to know here many chests of gold are buried on Thomas Barrett's land, near Scantic Falls. They have declared their good faith by placing s $100 government bond in Mr. Barrett's hands, and have set workmen to digging, promising to share with the town, the poor, and the owner of the land. Searches for gold have been made here before, but they claim to have found the right place.*

By January 27th a reporter from the Springfield Republican showed some initiative and took it upon himself to gain firsthand knowledge of the excavation, the miner, and his mission.

> *Here, then, the rainbow ends, and at last the pot of gold is sure to be found.*

> *The quiet Scantic is bordered by many low hills graced with a slender growth of oak saplings and scrubby pines, which find slight nourishment in the shallow gravel, and in the side of one of these hills, rather more than half a mile from Hazardville, a singular enthusiast is mining under spirt for hidden treasures.*

> *Following a road across the meadows well worn by his many curious visitors, I reached what is called the 'Scitico Gold Mine', a few feet above the riverbed a rod distant; and there, swinging down into the irregular excavation he has made, I found a man.*

The Scientific American has been in print since 1845 and is the oldest continuously published magazine in the United States.

CLAIRVOYANTS.

SADIE JOHNSON—Medical and business clairvoyant; tells of lost property; absent friends, joins the separated; speaks of love and marriage. family troubles and future events; gives magnetic treatment and medicated ba hs; heals the sick; call on her before going elsewhere and test her power; 37 Tremont st.

"AN HOUR WITH THE ASTROLOGER." Prof. GREGGS of New York will be at the Adams House, 555 Washington st., Monday, Oct. 18. Chart of planets at your birth, with judgment upon health, business, matrimony, family matters.

WE RECOMMEND MRS. BOUTELLE on business a fairs, love, marriage absent friends, lost property, and all diseases; gives names, brings separated together, and te ls your life from the cradle to the grave; letters, $1; 770 Washington st.

GRACE ROYAL—The wonderful test, business and medical medium: gives names, prospects, losses, future, love, marr age, etc., 52½ Beach street.

MME. FORESTIA—63 Hancock st., opposite the reservoir, new trill baths and magnetic treatment; will be found the very best in the city.

MME. BISHOP—Mind reader, having just returned from Europe, invites her friends to call at old residence, 7 Ohio st., near Indiana place.

MME. LEE—Clairvoyant de Paris; best in city; medicated sponge baths and magnetic treatment; 210 Eliot st.; 1 flight; don't ring.

MME. WILLETT—Only French clairvoyant in Boston; 41 Howard st.; room 5; 9 A.M. to 12 P.M.

MARTHA HANSON—Clairvoyant Francais, 116 Court st., 1 flight, room 5; home day & evening.

AT 165 PLEASANT ST., Room 1, MME. ALVARDI gives magnetic treatment, sponge baths.

MABEL WEST AND MISS CARRIE—Clairvoyants; 687 Washington st.; up 2 flights.

MADAME FANCHON—Sponge baths; room 5, 165 Pleasant st.; 1 flight front; don't ring.

MME. MYERS—Vapor baths and magnetic treatment; 33 Motte st., cor. Washington st.

MME. REYNOLDS—Clairvoyant, magnetic healer; 210 Eliot st.; 1 flight; don't ring.

SADIE, GEORGIA & MAY—Clairvoyants; best in the city; 79 Green st.; from Maine.

NELLIE SWAIN—Clairvoyant, 857 Washington street, 1 flight. Remember the number.

MISS LUTHER—Magnetic physician; treatments $1, 86 Essex st., up one flight.

ANNIE OAKES—44 Pleasant st , 1 flight; home Sunday and evenings; fortunes told.

LENA GREENWOOD—Clairvoyant, 36 Lynde st., off Green; 1 flight; don't ring.

LITTLE ADA has returned to 36 Edinboro st.; from 9 to 4; home evenings.

EMMA ELLSWORTH—Clairvoyant, No. 8 Davis st.; home Sundays.

MISS EVANS—Magnetic treatment and sulphur bath, 198 Eliot street.

LUE ARLINGTON—906 Washington street; room 1; 9 to 7.

MISS FLORA PAGE—Clairvoyant, 198 Eliot street.

He was turning a drill for the strokes of a sledge, patiently confident that every blow brought him nearer to that long-sealed cave, with its two iron chests filled with unreckoned wealth. He spoke of it quite simply as a fact, and presently relieved by one of his workmen – he employs but two at present – Putnam came out.

The tall broad shouldered man, with curling brown hair and beard, keen face and merry eyes, utterly contradicted my expectations. I went to find a long-haired, unkempt, uncanny specimen, with wild eyes that would justify consignment to an insane asylum, for with that type of Spiritualists I was familiarized.

He was glad to tell his story, and the vagaries of his belief and purpose were given to me frankly as mere matters of fact.

'No, I don't work for the treasure' he said, 'but for the truth. My individual band of spirits – and Benjamin Franklin as the head of them – want me to test the power of the clairvoyant spirits in the upper world. They say there is a treasure here; perhaps they are mistaken, - Franklin can't tell; I can't tell. But anyway, I shall get the truth.'

And so, he told me his story.

A.W. Putnam is of the Israel Putnam stock, though not a lineal descendent of the old hero. For fourteen years he has lived in California, most of the time as a farmer, and, as he says, under impressions from spirits, invented a labor-saving machine, which he came east to introduce.

Having seen time and money wasted in haphazard prospecting after gold, he studied clairvoyance as a means of locating mines with accuracy and thinks he has mastered the natural laws governing that faculty. Reaching Boston the attendant spirits sent him to McKean County, PA., to determine a coal mine. He stopped at Hartford on the way to see a medium there, who gave him in the clairvoyance trance a panoramic view of the Scantic, and described to him the burning of the two pirate ships at the mouth of the Connecticut; the escape up the river of fourteen Spaniards in two boats; their reaching some falls in the Scantic; their sanguinary fight with the Indians, and the death of seven of their number; the carrying of two iron chests laden with treasure, into a long narrow cave by the remaining seven, and their departure.

Proceeding to Pennsylvania, he settled the place to mine for coal, but his spirit band advised him to try for the Spanish treasure first, because it was more easy of access and would be an equally good test.

He had never seen the place, but found it as pictured by the medium. He determined to leave everything to the guidance of Franklin and trusted him not in vain. A Boston man was influenced to furnish him money to dig, and at his lodgings in Scitico he found a young man in whose hands the witch hazel would indicate the presence of water [dowsing]. With him he explored the designated spot, assured that if the spirits had guided this matter, they would make the hazel bend towards the metal as well. His instructions then were, to dig away the gravel to the level of the root of a particular hickory sapling, and to drill a flat rock he would then reach at a central spot which the hazel pointed out, and after he had blasted out rock to a depth of three feet, the next charge he put in would explode down instead of up.

'And there I thought I should find the cave,' he parenthesized, 'but that was only my inference; the spirits didn't say so.'

Then the hazel rod sent him some five feet in an easterly direction, and he said, 'I was fool enough to expect to find the cave there; the spirits didn't tell me so.' Reaching that point, the hazel changed his course again, and he is now on the way to his third stake, six feet and seven inches northerly.

His hope of terminating his search at that point is strengthened by the peculiar action of the magic hazel, which is now attracted to an oval space inside of which there is no special center of magnetic force.

The original entrance to the cave was at the northeast of the hill and has been so closed by the settling and crumbling of the rock that an attempt to find it would be futile. The Hartford clairvoyant came out to the spot, and through him the spirits fixed the location of the former mouth just at the edge of an abandoned quarry, where the 'earth rings hollow below,' even now. He also pointed out s mound beneath an apple tree east of the hill as the grave of five of the Spaniards, and there Mr. Putnam is to erect a monument when the chests are disclosed, and meanwhile, by command of the spirits, has marked the spot by five stones.

Mr. Putnam has no acquaintance with any spiritualists in the neighborhood, and those of Somers do not appear to have taken any interest in his work. He thinks he will soon reach the chamber – in one week if the next point be the final one, and in the meantime, he takes no heed of Sundays, to the great scandalizing of the good people of the region. He calls his religion 'naturalism' and is not connected with any body of Spiritualists.

I have omitted to say that the rock he is excavating is a soft red sandstone of irregular cleavage, and has been used for building, though chiefly in cellar walls. He commenced digging the last day of December and professes to be quite astonished that anyone should have noticed his whim. 'Why' said he, 'I supposed they would say "He's a crazy man," and pass along, but, as it is it will be a sort of test, in folks' estimation, of the truth of spirit intercourse, and I don't quarrel with that. But if you say anything about me – I haven't the shadow of an objection – say the truth.

Men have sneaked around here and made-up stories from what they could piece together. I am glad you came straight to me.'

And here you have the gist of the Scitico excitement.

Frankly, I was interested in the man; his shrewd commonsense and quick with mingling strangely with his mania, and his hearty bonhomie with his philosophy of spirits, are to me a new study in human life.

And as to the pirates' gold and jewels, I have Mr. Putnam's word for it that I shall know when he has found them, and that is also the firm belief of [this author].

How disconcerting must it have been to the reporter to expect a madman and instead encounter someone wholly competent – except, possibly, for his Spiritualist beliefs in communicating with the dead. It certainly would have been easier to discount the treasure recovery adventure as a flight of fancy should the miner have presented as bereft of his senses, but to discuss the excavation as a "test" of sorts of his faith, moved the discussion to a new plane.

Were there some truths to the venture?

Was there the actual possibility of a pirate's treasure buried along the Scantic waterway?

Two days later a new article appeared in the January 29th edition of the Boston Investigator.

> *The parties from Boston [sic California], who, under alleged direction, have been digging at Scitico, Conn., in search of a cave full of hidden treasure, deposited there 300 years ago by 'pirates,' failed, as a matter of course, to come upon the expected $5,000,000 at the point designated, viz., the end of the lateral gallery running 'three feet southeast' from the bottom of a particular hole.*

> *The disappointment does not seem to have cured them of their delusion, for they are still at work blasting and digging for the five millions of hidden treasure.*

On February 4, 1868, an article in the San Francisco bulletin added certain particulars to the story. The labor-saving machine Putnam had invented was a corn planter, which he either patented himself or had sold to another who patented the equipment, walking away with $7000.

The article identified the medium who recounted the location of the buried treasure as a Miss Caswell of Boston, and the investor who provided the funds for the venture as a Mr. Doolan (a member of the Boston Common Council at the time). Doolan promised more funds should Putnam require them once he had exhausted the initial $5000.

The Boston Globe regularly ran advertisements for local

and regional clairvoyants, and a search including years bracketing that period returned no results for that name.

The work continued.

By March 28th the Columbia Register of New Haven reported the:

> *Spiritual gold diggers still hard at work on the Scantic river, picking, drilling, and blasting into the solid rock, some 20 feet below the surface of the earth. They have struck the walls of the treasure bearing cave, and as soon as they can penetrate to the interior, the bars of gold and chests of diamonds will be within their grasp.*
>
> *The 'medium' in Boston sends daily instructions for the prosecution of their work.*

Scantic River winding through Scitico, Enfield, CT., where pirate treasure waits for a lucky explorer.

On April 8th a small announcement appeared in the New Bedford Evening Standard reporting that:

> *The Scitico (CT.) gold digger has abandoned his Spanish treasure and vamoosed, whether under the influence of Franklin's spirit or not, is unknown. His tools are safe, as the cave he made is full of water. His bills are left, to some extent, unpaid, but as he has paid double prices the losses will be only half their face.*

And so, the adventure came to a quiet close, the treasure hunter and hired hands leaving the site without fanfare; the same way they had arrived.

But what if they had simply quit too soon?

Suppose they had been a mere five feet from breaking through to that cave where the millions of dollars of gold had been hidden?

Two feet?

One foot?

What if the Scitico Gold still lies waiting there in a cave on the side of a hill near the flowing Scantic for someone with a greater sense of commitment?

Greater faith?

Perhaps this story waits for a dreamer to pick up a pick and a shovel and write the last words of this chapter and surprise us all.

Might that be you?

3: SANITARIUM SECRETS

Why do people contemplate suicide?

Christin Cammarata discusses the subject in her article on teen suicide:

> *Most teens interviewed after making a suicide attempt say that they did it because they were trying to escape from a situation that seemed impossible to deal with or to get relief from really bad thoughts or feelings. They didn't want to die as much as they wanted to escape from what was going on. And at that particular moment dying seemed like the only way out.*

> *Some people who end their lives or attempt suicide might be trying to escape feelings of rejection, hurt, or loss. Others might feel angry, ashamed, or guilty about something. Some people may be worried about disappointing friends or family members.*

> *What makes a person unable to see another way out*

of a bad situation besides ending their life? [60]

Before World War I, upper-class gay men and lesbians were accepted into the highest levels of Boston society without so much as a raised eyebrow.

Homosexuality was simply social background noise.

After the War ended in 1918 though, a shift in public attitudes toward homosexuality brought an end to the tolerance and started a series of purges and police actions that lasted through 1920.

The *Secret Court of 1920* was a disciplinary tribunal consisting of five administrators at Harvard University that was created to investigate charges of homosexual activity among the student population.

For two weeks spanning the months of May and June 1920, the Court, which was led by Chester Noyes Greenough, the acting dean, conducted more than 30 clandestine interviews.

Students who confessed to homosexual behavior were permanently expelled.

Those who did not were either exonerated or allowed to come back to Harvard after a year or two of forced leave.

For those who were summarily expunged from the university the Dean sent letters to the students' parents, outlining the behavior that led to their sons' expulsions.

At the conclusion of the hearings a total of seven young men were expelled.

---

[60] Cammarata, Christine. Suicide. 2020.

My dear ▮▮▮▮▮▮:

It is with the deepest regret that I inform you that your son, ▮▮▮▮▮▮, has involved himself in difficulties so extraordinarily great that the President has directed me to advise him to withdraw from The University at once. I have communicated these instructions to your son and he is leaving. He has promised me to tell you all about the matter, and I am confident that he will do so, if indeed he has not done so already.

His difficulties are, in brief, somewhat as follows. A certain group of Harvard students, in connection with a group of older men in Boston, have been guilty of homosexual practices, and one of the men deeply involved is your son's roommate. Your son, though we believe him to be innocent of any homosexual act, is in the following ways too closely connected with those who have been guilty of these acts.

An excerpt from an actual letter written to one of the students from the Harvard Court.

An eighth committed suicide, evading the "justice" of the Court.

A teaching assistant and professor were fired.

Two students who were found guilty of tolerating gay behavior were suspended for between one to three years.

As if those actions were not punishment enough, letters were also placed in the students' permanent files so the explicit reason for their expulsion was communicated to admissions officers is they applied to alternate schools.

Potential employers were informed as to why these young men were expelled.

As a result, the men never graduated from any college and were forced into unconventional careers [61].

This was not a unique situation for homosexual men who were outed or publicly exposed in the prurient 1920's in New England.

Men's lives were basically ruined.

Isolated as if they were harboring a type of contagion.

---

[61] Paley, Armit R. The Secret Court of 1920. 2002.

Edwin Smith Vail was born to Edmund and Martha Wodell (Husted) Vail in Union Vale, Duchess County, New York, on February 29th, 1860, a leap year baby.

As a young man Edwin attended the New York Homeopathic Medical College in New York City. The school had been founded in 1860 by William Cullen Bryant, poet and editor of the Evening Post, who believed that medicine should be practiced with a greater sensitivity to the needs of patients.

Bryant himself was zealously devoted to the branch of medicine known as homeopathy, which advocated moderation in medicinal dosage, exercise, a good diet, fresh air, and rest in treating illness.

In 1875, the Homeopathic Hospital (later renamed to the Metropolitan Hospital when it was relocated to Blackwell's Island) opened as a municipal facility on Ward's Island and was staffed largely by the faculty and students at New York Medical College. As a point of reference Ward's Island (conjoined with Randall's Island) are separated from Manhattan to the west by the Harlem River, from Queens to the east by the East River, and north from the Bronx by the Bronx Kill.

Following his graduation in 1882, Edwin Vail worked at the Homeopathic Hospital providing services to patients in the psychopathic ward of that institution. It was a sobering experience and only proved to validate his choice of vocation.

Two years after graduation, in 1884, Edwin married Sarah Tilson in Highland, Ulster County, New York. The pair first settled in Litchfield, Connecticut, moving shortly thereafter to Wallingford, Connecticut, where they welcomed daughter Ethel into their lives on February 20th of 1885, only to sadly bid her farewell after two days.

The New York Homeopathic Medical College and Hospital. New York Historical Society, Robert L. Bracklow Photograph Collection.

Thornton, the couple's first son, was born 23 months later in January of 1887.

At this point records are mixed as to the exact date that the Vails moved from Wallingford to Enfield, Connecticut, where Edwin would open his medical facility.

The Report of the State of Charities, [62] published in 1905, recorded the opening of the Vail Sanitarium in 1888, in a red brick building owned by the good doctor on Enfield Street.

Conversely the New Haven Register recorded the doctor as not even having purchased the building until 1890, two years past the date cited by the State Charities publication. In an announcement in the New Haven paper in September of 1890 the article noted the purchase

...of a line brick home by Dr. E. S. Vail in Enfield

---

[62] Public Documents of the State of Connecticut. 1905 Part 2.

*where he will engage more extensively in the treatment
of nervous diseases.*

In any event, most publications agree that the sanitarium
was open and operating out of the family home by 1890.
The New Haven Register noted in an announcement in
their June 6th, 1891, edition that:

*Dr. E. S. Vail was in town yesterday for a short
visit. He is having all the business he cares to do at
his sanitarium in Enfield.*

Ensconced in the town and quite successful, the Vails
welcomed their second son, Ramon Montgomery Vail, into
their happy home in May of 1893.

Their happiness once again was short lived though as
Sarah, his wife of ten years, passed away from an
undisclosed illness on May 15 of 1894, leaving the doctor
alone with two infants and a burgeoning business.

Twelve months later, finding his social footing, the New
Haven Journal Courier announced of the engagement of
Dr. Vail to Anna Stanley King of Enfield, the daughter of
Reverend Horace King.

The two were wed that August.

By 1903 Vail's practice had outgrown his home hosting
inmates for his sanitarium, and work on a new 18 room
building on the same Enfield Street property had begun.
The Springfield Republican noted:

*Work on the foundation for the new sanitarium to be
built by Dr. Edwin S. Vail on Enfield Street was
begun yesterday by a force of men in charge of Andrew
Tryon. The plans for the building were drawn by Isaac
A. Allen, Jr., of Hartford, and they call for a
structure of handsome design.*

Elmcroft (Vail) Sanitarium, Enfield, Connecticut.

The site selected for the sanitarium is one of the most beautiful on Enfield Street, commanding an unobstructed view from all sides.

For years the doctor and staff provided care for the mentally challenged. As the Hartford Courant noted while reporting on a once-in-four-year birthday celebration held at the site in 1907:

> *Elmcroft [the formal name of the Vail facility] is certainly not only a place for rest and recuperation, but with its buildings of high order is an ornament and credit to the town. Situated on the crest of "Enfield Street" with extensive views in each direction, it is a fortunate selection for a home of this kind.*

On November 1st, 1919, an unnamed inmate escaped from the Vail Sanitarium.

Inmates had escaped before, but what made this event of particular interest was the refusal of Dr. Vail to disclose the identity of the individual, even to the police departments of the region, let alone the newspapers.

Local authorities were asked to be on the lookout for a man of 5 feet 10 inches, 35 to 40 years of age, weight of about 140 pounds, dark complexion wearing a light grey suit. As the Courant's reporter noted in the November 2nd edition:

> *Dr. Vail refused to say where the man came from or how he arrived at the sanitarium, and when it was suggested that he might be more easily be found if it were known [from] where he was, the doctor said that he could not give any information on the matter. It is said the man had been at the sanitarium little more than a week and made his getaway during the morning. It is said that he is a man of considerable means and that every effort will be made to locate him*

and have him returned to the sanitarium before his relatives are advised that he is missing. Inasmuch as the Hartford police were notified of his disappearance, it is thought here that he undoubtedly is familiar with this city if not a resident here and might attempt to make his way here.

The Courant followed up in an article the following day, only adding to the enigma.

Mystery Shrouds Name of Missing patient Who Fled Vail Sanitarium

The offering of a reward of $500 for information leading to the apprehension of the male inmate of Vail's Sanitarium in Enfield, who disappeared from the institution Saturday morning has flung a veritable cloak of mystery about the entire case. Offering of the substantial reward linked with the absolute refusal of Dr. Edwin S. Vail to disclose the identity of the man heightens the mystery.

Even to the police Dr. Vail has maintained his attitude of profound secrecy.

By November 4th the doctor continued his silence.

"Mum" is still the word regarding the identity of the missing male patient who disappeared from the Vail Sanitarium in Enfield Saturday morning. All efforts to determine from persons, who are a position to know, the name of the man, his residence, or anything more than a description, have proved fruitless.

By the 4th of November regional papers had identified the missing patient despite the efforts of Dr. Vail to maintain the anonymity of the inmate. The Thompsonville

Press reported:

> *The missing patient from the Vail Sanitarium on Enfield Street, according to Hartford papers, is Samuel F. Crowell, of Manchester, manager of the Hartford agency of the Library Bureau on Pearl Street.*
>
> *Crowell was brought to the Vail Sanitarium three weeks ago by relatives and was assigned to a room on the third floor. He was suffering from a nervous breakdown.*
>
> *Early last Saturday morning, he disappeared after requesting the nurse to bring him his breakfast to his room.*
>
> *He slipped on his outer clothing, overcoat, shoes, and hat, but failed to take either socks or underwear.*

Samuel Fuller Crowell was well known in Hartford, and was a member of the University Club, having graduated from a Western college [Wesleyan University] in the class of 1902, [and earlier from the Boston Latin School in 1898]. He was a member of the Phi Nu Theta fraternity of the college.

At 40 years of age, Crowell was a single man, living with his uncle Albert L. Crowell in Highland Park, Manchester, Connecticut, for the 11 years since he had moved to the area from Boston in 1908.

On his draft registration card, completed one year prior to his disappearance, he had cited his next of kin, surprisingly, as his mother, Susan Grimsly Blodgett Crowell, not his uncle, whose address he had provided as his primary residence and with whom he lived.

His mother had graduated from the New England Conservatory of Music, and had entered the teaching profession, marrying Samuel Fuller Crowell Sr., a banker, in 1875. Her husband had passed away 5 months before

Crowell's military draft registration card of 1918.

his son's birth in 1879, leaving the youth with no father figure during his formative years and fomenting what some might have considered an uncomfortable attachment to his mother.

As the son of a single parent Crowell nonetheless excelled at the all-boys Boston Latin School, the oldest such school in America, founded in 1635. Reflective of his personality he had earned honors there for "Exemplary Conduct and Punctuality" while others had been recognized for their "Excellence in Classics, Modern Studies, Reading, and Written Exercises".

Perhaps due to his penchant for exactitude, Samuel, upon graduation, took a job as a salesman with the Library Bureau at their headquarters in Boston. Popular among his peers and admired by his employer for his meticulousness, he rose to the position of sales manager.

The Library Bureau had been founded by Melville Dewey in 1876. The company president was broadly recognized for his Dewey Decimal System, and his firm provided supplies and equipment to libraries to help enforce the same structure to the visual presentation of books as his system had done for publication filing and retrieval.

In 1908 Crowell was reassigned to Hartford as Manager of the Library Bureau branch on Main Street in the capital city, the previous manager having been transferred to the newly opened San Francisco branch. He quickly acclimated himself, joining the University Club of Hartford, an all-male social club, and, as the Hartford Courant noted:

He was known as a "live wire" in community activities.

In the publication Morals, Manners, Business and Civics, Samuel Fuller Crowell, writing an article on *The Card System*, might well have been writing about himself.

Being systematic in the keeping and arrangement of one's things is largely a matter of personal make-up, or "disposition", as we call it. To some fortunate individuals it comes as natural to have the "place for everything" with the right thing in it, as for others to have the place, but with everything in it. The latter have to acquire by training and education what is missing – namely, the habit of being systematic.[63]

Regimentation served Crowell well as he assumed the position of Corporal in the reserve company of Company F of the State Guard of Connecticut and was equally active in the Red Cross.

Crowell's public persona reflected a steady and consistent man of moral fiber, at times bordering on the boring. Consider the stirring presentation reported in the New Britain Herald that he gave to the commercial classes of the Grammar School of that city on *"The History of Filing"*. The newspaper noting that "his lecture proved to be interesting as well as instructive to the pupils."

The University Club was organized in 1906 at 30 Lewis Street in the state capital and was the club to join for those who could not afford the more prestigious Hartford Club. Promoted as a place where there would be a "maximum of good fellowship with a minimum of expense," it reflected a less pretentious and more youthful vibe. As one prominent member reflected:

I go to the Hartford Club for a business reason or to attend a trustees meeting, but I go to the University Club to see my friends and have fun.[64]

The membership included a fair share of bachelors who, according to reports, were not in any financial position to get married yet. In addition to the benefits of socialization the club was open seven days a week and served three meals a day.

---

[63] Welsh, C. (1918). Draper's Self Culture: Morals, manners, business and civics.

[64] Grant, E. S. (1984). The Club on Prospect Street.

PROGRAM

C'est a rire.

Finale, "I'm back."

INTERMISSION.

An ad for the Library Bureau in the University Club of Hartford's show Minstrels at Unity Hall in 1909.

In their heyday, the private men's clubs of the capital city were the opulent sites for Hartford's social scene, the

94

stomping grounds of Hartford's society, celebrity, academia, and professionals.

Among them, the University Club earned a reputation as a place that was far more entertaining than its staider counterparts The Hartford Club on Prospect Street, The Hartford Golf Club in West Hartford, and the Town and Country Club on Hartford's Woodland Street.

Crowell's more protected personal persona fit right in.

By November 6th a statewide search had begun for the missing man with search parties scouring the woods from Thompsonville to Somers to Manchester.

The $500 reward was drawing a small army to the region in hopes of locating both the man and collecting the bounty.

Rumors ran wild as to sightings of the escaped inmate. In the Hartford Courant November 6th edition:

> *R. L Taylor, proprietor of the Taylor Market at the corner of Charter Oak and Main Street, who has known Crowell for a number of years said yesterday that [at] about 8 o'clock Monday morning [November 3] he was passing Globe Hollow Pond and saw a man nude bathing. He thought it queer that anyone should be bathing at this particular time of year but did not tell anyone of his observations until yesterday morning, when after reading the story in the Courant of the Crowell case, he said he recalled that the man he saw looked very much as Crowell did the last time he saw him.*

By November 8th the Connecticut State Guard announced they would take up the search for the missing inmate as well. Colonel Charles Burpee of the State Guard sent out a request to all members of Company F and

Reserve Company F, of which Crowell had been an active member as a lieutenant at that time, to congregate in Enfield and Manchester to begin a systematic search for the missing man. The directive was to search the woods and swamps to from the west of the sanitarium up to the banks of the Connecticut River.

Printed circulars carrying the likeness of Crowell had blanketed the area from Springfield, Massachusetts to Hartford, Connecticut.

Word circulated that if Edwin Crowell had not been located by the following Monday that the Library Bureau would begin combing the entire country.

The Courant article continued:

> *A net of peculiar circumstances surrounds the disappearance of Crowell. At the time he left the institution, Dr. Thornton Vail was in charge of the sanitarium in the absence of his father, Dr. Edwin Vail. Wednesday Dr. Vail left the sanitarium. Yesterday his brother R. Raymond Vail, who was left in charge with his father and brother away, left the institution and all inquiries have failed to secure information as to where he has gone. Attendants and nurses alike cannot say when any of the three doctors will return.*

> *By Sunday the 9th, the eighth day since Crowell's disappearance, the State Guard completed their search of the area east of the sanitarium in failure.*

> *Spreading out in a skirmish formation nearly one hundred members of Company F and Reserve Company F of the State Guard yesterday searched territory covering over three-square miles directly east of the Vail Sanitarium from which Samuel F.*

> *Crowell, manager of the Library Bureau of this city, mysteriously disappeared a week ago yesterday. Results of the search were not encouraging, and the guardsmen returned from the search dog-tired from wading through marshland, swamps, and underbrush, of which the territory is largely composed.*
>
> *Included in the search party were members of the Library Bureau as well as members of the University Club.*

At the same time, Frank Luckingham of 16 Pleasant Street, Enfield, scoured the shores of the Connecticut River from Springfield to Middletown in his motorboat, to no avail.

The New Britain Herald did report that Luckingham had recovered a soft felt hat from the Colt breakwater that was thought to belong to Crowell, although ownership couldn't be determined.

It began to look as if the young man had indeed taken his own life, possibly in the Connecticut River, a view shared by the Thompsonville Press in their November 20th, 1919, edition.

Seven months passed.

On June 27, 1920, the Hartford Courant buried an article on page forty-two referencing a reaction to a recent Hartford Times report concerning the missing inmate.

Buncombe [65] *is Verdict on Vail Interview*

Dr. Joseph Root, Friend of Missing Samuel F.

---

[65] nonsense

Crowell, Denounces Sanitorium Proprietor's Dark Secret.

For the first time Dr. Edwin Vail had publicly alluded to a "dark secret" Samuel Fuller Crowell had carried with him long before escaping the sanitarium in 1919.

Dr. Vail said in his interview printed in the Hartford Times that Mr. Crowell "had no mental affliction." The sanitarium proprietor said that, in order to prevent unpleasantness coming to a number of friends, Samuel F. Crowell went away.

What "unpleasantness" could have included several of Crowell's acquaintances? What information, if divulged, might have impacted any number of his friends in a negative and possibly controversial way?

Perhaps the musings of Crowell's friend Dr. Root suggested a possibility as he discussed the peculiarities of Samuel Fuller Crowell in the body of the same article.

I know Sam Crowell as few other men did. Time and again I have camped with him; we have lived together.

There were few men who were more particular about their attire than Sam Crowell.

Even in the wilderness he took the greatest care with his cravat [66]. Of course, he wore an outing shirt, but he still had his cravat faultlessly arranged.

He shaved daily.

He was very careful of his personal appearance.

Now, do you mean to tell me, that a man who has always exhibited these traits would go away, possibly

---

[66] Historical necktie. A short, wide strip of fabric worn by men around the neck and tucked inside an open-necked shirt.

on a long trip, without his stockings?

No man who desired to appear natty even in the wilds would – if he were entirely sane – care to travel through a civilized community as was Sam Crowell at the time of his disappearance.

Sam Crowell, as I knew him, would not have taken Dr. Vail and only Dr. Vail into his confidence in an affair of this sort.

He idolized his mother. Surely, he did not think more of Dr. Vail than he did of his mother.

But take the doctor into his confidence he had, and perhaps Vail was showing the young man, missing now for many long months, the greatest kindness by not revealing the one truth that saved the social embarrassment of his friends in 1920 while at the same time reducing Crowell's options to one.

Dr. Edwin Vail at Elmcroft (EHS Collection).

If the dark secret were to have been publicly revealed, or even had been threatened to be revealed, then his professional life might well have been over.

On August 29th, 1920, a full 10 months after his disappearance, the body of Samuel Fuller Crowell was discovered floating in the Connecticut River about five miles below the sanitarium by two youths, Arthur Pfeifer and Frank Wackford.

As Dr. Edwin Vail had once revealed to Captain Robert Hurley, of the Connecticut State Police, long before the young man's body had been recovered:

> ... *if Crowell were dead, this secret chapter, for the good of all concerned, had best be buried with him.*

When pressed for comment on the nature of the "secret" Hurly reflected:

> *What this secret chapter of Crowell's life is I do not know. Dr. Vail knows, and I suppose that the many others alleged to be involved know about it. It must have been a serious matter as it evidently brought about the young man's death.*

> *This secret will evidently go to his grave with him.*

> *I [know] that it preyed upon him to the point where he had considered suicide for some time.*

> *He went to Atlantic City and there, while on a trip for his health, couldn't forget this secret and tried to commit suicide in a bathtub. He failed in that attempt.*

> *He told Dr. Vail about this [episode] and when he came to the Vail Sanitarium, he promised he would not attempt to take his life again.*

> *Whether his death has made this matter a closed incident time alone will tell.*

The story had captured the attention of the region for almost a year based on the initial mystery surrounding the identity of the inmate, the sizable reward that had been offered, and the interest of the public in what kind of personal demon it would take to drive a man to remove himself from the public eye and ultimately from life itself.

Rumors swirled.

One last bit of information came to light over the following days.

Of the few items Sam Crowell had taken with him during his escape, besides the spare clothing, was a letter from his mother, which was found in the breast pocket of his coat, positioned over his heart.

The musings of his mother had become blurred due to exposure to the ice and water of the Connecticut River, so the words could not be read nor the content determined.

And perhaps that was for the best.

4: BA DA BOOM

Giuseppe (Joseph) Napolitano was born in Napoli (Naples), Campania, Italy in 1868. One of two boys, unusual for an Italian family of that time, he and his brother Salvatore had an uneventful childhood.

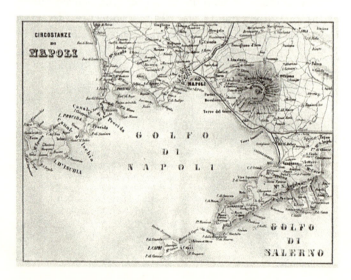

Map of Napoli, Italy (Published by Ronchi, Milano Italy 1870)

Two years after his birth, in 1870, the Italian Army took control of both Rome and the Papal States, as France was deeply involved in the Franco-Prussian War and had removed their garrison from Rome. The Italian peninsula was unified under the Kingdom of Italy.

The country was a violent place as most men owned guns, and crime was rampant. Of the 3,000 murders per year, many were the result of cyclical conflicts between families or gangs. Organized associations were active in the southern regions of the mainland, and revenge killings were commonplace.

By 1890 Giuseppe had married Cecilia Mascola, a small Sicilian woman of four feet nine inches tall, and the two began their family in 1893, in Casamarciano, with the birth of their first son, Saboto in 1893. Three years later their first daughter Giovanna was born, and like clockwork, in another three years, son Pasquale arrived in 1899.

In March of 1905 Giuseppe emigrated to the United States aboard the S.S. Algeria [67], joining his cousin in New York City for a short time.

Cecilia and his children emigrated to the United States two years later, in 1907 [68], with a destination of Springfield, Massachusetts noted on their immigration papers.

Records are unclear as to why Giuseppe had relocated to Springfield, Massachusetts from New York, but it can be safely assumed that work had something to do with it, as the 1910 census records indicate Giuseppe was a laborer without a specific industry attached to his trade.

By 1885, the Springfield Republican estimated that there

---

[67] S.S. Algeria passenger list arriving Ellis Island NY March 1905

[68] Venezia passenger list arriving Ellis Island NY November 1907

were 100 Italians living in Springfield with many working on the expanding road system which began to link the city center with the adjacent developing residential neighborhoods, or on the many commercial, municipal, and residential construction projects in the "City of Homes".

The Republican newspaper's 1875 headline for an article about the Italians of the South End read:

They Cluster Along the River Bank in Lieu of the Adriatic. [69]

Clearly opportunities were calling tradespeople and laborers to western Massachusetts, and the Napolitano's comfortably settled into a routine at their rented house at 71 Wilcox Street. Giuseppe and Cecilia welcomed son Michael in 1908 followed by daughter Marie in 1910, completing their family at three boys and two girls.

By 1917 Saboto [Sabot/Samuel], 23 years of age, had secured a position with the New England Telephone & Telegraph Company as a lineman, quite an accomplishment for a young man whose formal education had stopped at the sixth grade. A single man, he was living with his parents in the family home at 36 Fremont Street in Springfield.

Pasquale, 17 years old, was working as a Soda Clerk employed by the Louis Kroh Liggett Company, the largest cooperative drug manufacturing and selling organization in the world at that time. [70] Pasquale, Patsy as he was referred to by friends and acquaintances, or Patrick as he was recorded in the 1920 U. S. Census, lived at home with his family as well. The living arrangements spoke to the need for everyone to financially support their family as his

---

[69] Carvalho, Italians in Western Massachusetts The First Generations

[70] Financial Giants of America. Page 367

brother Saboto noted on his draft registration card that:

Mother depends somewhat on me. [71]

By 1920 the brothers had moved out of the family home and were listed as "lodgers" in the house of James Carlo at 38 Winthrop Street in the same city, less than ¼ mile from the home of their parents. Like their father, the homeowner James was an Italian laborer, who more than likely shared the values of Giuseppe and Cecilia Napolitano. Primarily an Italian neighborhood, the block included Russians, Germans, Canadians, and Irish; a true melting pot.

Sabot seemed to have moved again in 1921, one door over to 40 Winthrop, [72] while Patsy remained at the Carlo home.

What events occurred in the lives of the Napolitano's between the years of 1921 and 1925? Somehow, Patsy, a soda jerk at a corner drugstore became knowledgeable enough about pyrotechnics to start his own fireworks company, compete against the region's best, and win fireworks display contracts.

As recorded in a national magazine:

New England Fireworks Mfg. & Display Co., Inc., Springfield, Mass. 500 shares of no-par value stock, P. Napolitan, Pres., S. Napolitan, Tres., J. Napolitan. Secy., 524 Union St., Springfield, Mass. [73]

There were no other local companies from which Napolitano could have learned the skills, so how the young man acquired the expertise with and understanding about

---

[71] WWI United States Draft Registration Card (1917).

[72] U.S. City Directories 1822-1995 (Springfield, Massachusetts 1921)

[73] Chemical & Metallurgical Engineering. Volume 32 (1925)

pyrotechnics and the required rocketry is a mystery.

There was though, a few years earlier, another Massachusetts company with a similar name established in the Boston area, the New England Fireworks Company. That firm had been formally incorporated in 1912 in Winchester, Massachusetts, with Giuseppe Carlomagno [Carlemagne] as president, Vincent Brogna as treasurer, and Ernest [Ernesto] Borrelli [Borelli] as manager. Borrelli had owned and worked the establishment himself prior to selling out to Carlomagno. Giuseppe had originally viewed Borrelli's pyrotechnic display in East Boston while acting as toastmaster at the Blessed Virgin of Mount Carmel event and was impressed enough to purchase the operation.

Carlomagno, who also owned a business importing Italian olive oil located near Union Station in Boston, had purchased a safe from Raffaelle Collaruso, another Italian immigrant from the neighborhood, to stash the funds he would use to buy the fireworks company.

That was where Carlomagno almost made a fatal misstep. He had never changed the combination to the secondhand safe, and Collaruso knew he had not. It was only by luck one evening that Carlomagno came home unexpectedly to find Collaruso kneeling in front of the safe, twisting the dial in hopes of running off with the businessman's money.

Startled, Collaruso had rushed the homeowner while brandishing a razor, which Carlomagno dodged, knocking the assailant down, and holding him until police arrived.

An early crisis averted.

The New England Fireworks Company manufactured explosives and rockets for local and regional celebrations in a one-story wooden building of 30 by 60 feet. Carlomagno employed three men in the enterprise besides Borrelli; Frederico Gennani who was 31 years old and single, Luigi Francis, 28 and single, and Giuseppe Musta, 29 years old and married.

The business thrived until the afternoon of July 19th,

1913, when the town of Winchester was shaken for a ten-mile radius as the fireworks manufactory was, in the words of the Boston Globe headline – *Blown to Splinters* – leaving nothing but a crater where the small production facility had once stood.

Ernest Borrelli, the manager and Italian immigrant who had settled in Winchester in 1908, had been lifted into the air by the explosion and had landed 20 feet away. Dazed and confused he meandered ¼ mile until dropping into some bushes, where he was found more than one hour later.

The three other employees had been severely burned and were taken to a local hospital for treatment. Musta sustained a hole in the side of his body, where he had been struck by a rocket. [74] He was initially listed in critical condition but would survive. The other two employees were treated and released, as was Borrelli, after he had been found.

It was reported that the company applied for a permit to rebuild in another section of town, but that request was denied, and Borelli disappeared into history.

Carlomagno though retained his import business for years and never dabbled in pyrotechnics again.

In 1915 the New England Fireworks Company was dissolved as a viable business by the Boston General Court.

Despite the similarity in name, it seems to have no known connection to either the New England Fireworks Mfg. & Display Co., Inc. of Springfield, Massachusetts, or the Napolitano's.

By January 21, 1926, a mere two months after their incorporation was publicly announced,

---

[74] Boston Sunday Post, July 20, 1913. Page 1.

A display of fireworks was given near the plant of the New England Fireworks Manufacturing Company, located on Brainard Road in the northeast section of the town last Sunday. [75]

By June 24 of that same year the fledgling company was beginning to enter competitions to capture contracts based on their pyrotechnical acumen. One enjoinment was announced in The Thompsonville Press in a page one article.

St. Cologero Festivities Will Open Saturday

Annual Two-Day Celebration by the Italian Residents Will Be Featured by Band Concerts, Parades, and a Big Display of Fireworks on Sunday.

The celebration Sunday night will conclude with a display of fireworks on the Park Avenue ball grounds. The fireworks companies will participate in a contest for the best display, one to be by the New England Fireworks Company of this village and the other by a New York company. [76]

The reviews and results were reported in the following week's edition of the same paper.

Fireworks Closes Big Italian Celebration

The New England Fireworks Company was awarded the decision in the competitive exhibition with a fireworks company of New Jersey. Both companies put on a remarkable display, but the novelties introduced by the local company which included a large picture in colored fire of St. Cologero, and a boy encircling the grounds on a bicycle, which

---

[75] The Thompsonville Press. January 21, 1926 edition. Page 4.
[76] The Thompsonville Press. June 24, 1926 edition. Page 1.

*burned for several minutes, gave the edge to the local
company.*

By July 22nd the local pyrotechnic firm was prepared to
put on the show for the annual Feast of Mt. Carmel, but at
the last moment the festivities were postponed due to rain
and high winds until the following Sunday.

Newspaper reports validated the company's selection.

*In the evening at 8:30 o'clock a band concert was
given on the Park Avenue ball grounds, followed by
a fine display of fireworks by the New England
Fireworks Manufacturing Co., which was witnessed
by several thousand people from this and the
surrounding towns.*[77]

His business firmly established, Patsy married Lucy
Anzalotti, a local girl from Enfield, at Saint Patrick's Church
on September 29, 1927. Guests from Springfield,
Worcester, and Boston, Massachusetts, attended as well as
many from New York City, Hartford and New Haven,
Connecticut.

After a reception at the Grand Army Hotel on State
Street in Springfield, Massachusetts, the couple left on a
wedding trip to Buffalo, Niagara Falls, Detroit, Michigan,
and New York City – a rather eclectic mix of locations. On
their return the new couple settled into Patsy's home at 37
Plymouth Street in Springfield.

The relationship between Napolitano and the residents
of Thompsonville continued to be supportive as well as
entertaining. The pyrotechnic company treated the

---

[77] The Thompsonville Press. July 28, 1927 edition. Page 1.

townspeople to a display of fireworks on January 9th of 1928 as they tested new rocket designs and set pieces at their plant. It was a delightful mid-winter break for residents.

To refer to the New England Fireworks Company production facilities as a *manufactory* would be an extreme misuse of the term. The operation consisted of eight 9 x 12, 8-foot-high wooden buildings, with roofs of sheet tin, widely scattered to prevent disaster from spreading from one to another should an explosion occur. Only one building housed volatile gunpowder. The others, except for the assembly building, were used for the storage of chemicals, tubes, and other items used in the manufacture of display sets, bombs, rockets, and aerial pieces.

From time-to-time Patsy would employ friends and relatives during busy periods to supplement his regular production crew. These same individuals would purchase materials *at cost* from the facility to produce explosives for their own entertainment during holidays or to celebrate special events.

On June 17th, 1928, at around 8:30 in the morning, with the Fourth of July festivities rapidly approaching, Charles Chevalier opened the gate to the fireworks production facility to allow access to a car filled with three youths and two adults. Behind the wheel of the auto, was William Doreski, 19 years old, driving a car loaned to him by his brother, Alec. In the back seat were John Anzalotti, 11 years old, and his sibling Joseph, 14, each younger brothers of Lucy, the wife of Patsy Napolitano, President of the fireworks company.

Accompanying them was Rosario Sarno, 45 years old, the Anzalotti boys' uncle, who was employed at the Bigelow Carpet Company in Thompsonville. Sarno was the brother

111

of Vincenzo Sarno, a well-respected Thompsonville baker whose business had been located on Church Street in the same section of Enfield for years.

The identity of the fifth passenger was unknown and was even an unidentified suspect in later reports.

By 8:40 the group had parked their vehicle outside of the chemical shed and had entered the building after being given the key by Michael Napolitano, Patsy's brother, and manager of the site. By all accounts the group began to gather up the materials needed for assembling some fireworks for their own enjoyment on the upcoming holiday. It wasn't an unusual practice for the group to have done so as the scene had played out many times before and all were familiar with the potential risks. At most there were 10 to 15 pounds of loose gunpowder inside the chemical shed, not enough to alarm anyone.

In addition, once the group had assembled the necessary components the mixing of the volatile ingredients was to be done outside of the shed on a table dedicated to that task.

At 8:45, at a gas station almost two miles away from the fireworks production site, near the main highway, E. R. Judd fell to the ground as his building and the immediate area shook as if gripped by an earthquake.

Looking to the north he saw a huge cloud of smoke rising skyward.

At 363 Enfield Street, more than one mile from the fireworks site, John Parker's wife, Cora, held onto the kitchen counter as the entire house trembled. Realizing where the eruption had come from, she tore from her house and was the first resident to arrive at the scene of the accident.

HAROLD J. BROMAGE
ATTORNEY-AT-LAW
SULLIVAN BLOCK—PHONE 49A

THOMPSONVILLE, CONN.,
November 5th.
1 9 2 8.

Mr. Sabat Napolitan,
524 Union Street,
Springfield, Mass.
Dear Sir:

The parents of William
Doreski, who was killed at
the New England Fireworks Co.
on the morning of June 26th.,
have consulted me with reference
to a claim for damages against
the New England Fireworks Company.
I am advised that you are a part
owner of this company and would
suggest that you let me hear from
you at an early date or take the
matter up with your attorney.

HB:R   Very truly yours,

H Bromage.

There, near the gate which led from Pine Point Grove to the fireworks manufactory, Cora came upon a man wide-eyed and seemingly in a state of shock. His clothes were shredded, face blackened, and he repeatedly mumbled "I couldn't help it."

Farther into the woods Michael Napolitano, Annabelle Mole, Joseph Seros, and Charles Chevalier ran from the main assembly building toward the origin of the explosion.

Parts of the tin roof and walls were scattered for hundreds of feet and were lodged in the tops of trees 300 feet away.

Planks and Paris Green cans, silver powder cans and other containers were twisted and hurled in all directions, covering the ground with small piles of many-colored powders, which were soon picked up by the wind and carried in a snowstorm of red, green, and silver to the woods nearby.

A shoe, seared by flame and heat, with the sole partly torn off, lay on the ground near the place where the chemical shed [once] stood, and a belt with torn shreds of clothing attached was hanging from a tree 100 feet away.[78]

A rash of phone calls brought the police to the scene, who in turn called local doctors Michael J. Dowd and Henry Wilson Fancher.

Both physicians, however, found that nothing could be done for the victims as they were not only dead, but their dismembered bodies were scattered for hundreds of feet around the grounds.

Patrolman Charles Lockwood next arrived and took charge. He was joined later by First Selectman Edward Bromage who took steps for the immediate policing of the surroundings, and the gathering of the remains of the victims for identification. This was not an easy task as such portions of the bodies as could be found were badly mangled. The police, with the

---

[78] Hartford Courant. Four Are Killed In Explosion Of Fireworks. June 17, 1928. Page 2.

assistance of several citizens, succeeded however, in gathering the remains of all four victims so that it was possible to identify them.[79]

All four bodies were mangled beyond recognition, parts of the bodies were found hanging from tree branches and scattered within a radius of 50 yards from where the building stood.

Although the bodies and parts of bodies show[ed] but four dead, Charles Chevalier of 798 Main Street, Springfield, who opened the gate to admit the Studebaker car to the grounds shortly after 8, stated positively there were five in the car.[80]

So, what became of the fifth person who was spotted entering the site in the automobile with the others?

What of the blackened, disoriented, and frantic individual running from the scene that was happened upon by Cora Parker?

The police had assumed that the lack of a body or body parts was evidence enough that no fifth individual had been present at the scene. Even if there had been another individual at the fireworks factory that morning, he never came forward afterwards to add any clarity to the situation.

And how did a chemical shed, with at most 10 to 15 pounds of gunpowder inside, explode with enough force to completely tear apart four bodies and a building?

The same question was on the mind of Sabot Napolitano when he proposed that someone with a grudge against the company was behind the explosion. After all, pyrotechnics was a competitive industry and the fledgling company had

---

[79] The Thompsonville Press. June 28, 1928 edition. Page 1.
[80] The Springfield Republican. June 28, 1928 edition. Page 5.

recently won more than their fair share of contracts.

So much success and attention in a short amount of time that Patsy was regionally referred to as the *Fireworks King*.

Perhaps a message was being sent?

Or perhaps it was just bad luck.

Whatever the true reason for the explosion, the funeral and burial of the victims that followed on June 28th was an incredibly solemn and moving affair, the deaths casting a pall over the community.

> *Because of the awesome character of the tragedy, and out of sympathy with the deeply affected families of the deceased, the church was not only crowded to capacity, but hundreds of people lined the streets around the entrance to the edifice.*

> *The bodies were accompanied to the cemetery by the largest funeral cortege in years, and an immense throng of people lined the way to the burying ground to witness the procession.* [81]

The town collectively mourned.

But within weeks Vincenzo Sarno, popular Thompsonville baker and brother of Rosario, filed an untimely death suit against both the fireworks company and Pasquale Anzalotti, father of the two boys who had perished in the explosion. Sarno claimed that the company was negligent in allowing access to the pyrotechnic materials, and further claimed that the Anzalotti family was complicit in making fireworks in their home and in carrying materials there from the factory.

The suit was dismissed, but relationships were wounded

---

[81] The Thompsonville Press. June 28, 1928 edition. Page 1.

for a lifetime.

Thirteen quiet months passed and once again the town was rocked by another explosion on July 29, 1929.

Pasquale and a crew of men had been at work all day transporting rockets and other fireworks to be employed onsite at a celebration at the Mount Carmel Society that evening. By six o'clock the site had been vacated and the pyrotechnic show set up and ready to enchant the audience later in the evening at the Park Avenue grounds in Thompsonville.

At seven p.m. one of 17 small buildings erupted in flames, blowing apart the wooden structure which contained manufactured fireworks but no loose gunpowder.

Soon a large crowd had gathered at the site as well as the North Thompsonville fire department who went to work to extinguish flames in the heavily wooded area.

Unlike the explosive event the previous year, there was no known employee or guest at the location, so no reason was immediately identified for the destructive blast.

As before, Pasquale Napolitano theorized sabotage by someone with a grudge against the organization who had attempted to injure the company by blowing up the building, perhaps to shut down the Mt. Carmel event.

No one had been seen at the site before the explosion, and Napolitano could not provide any possible suspects.

To address the concerns of a worried community, and to attempt to manage potential disasters, the Town of Enfield, which included the Village of Thompsonville, passed a modification to their zoning regulations on April 30th of 1930:

SECTION 6 – INDUSTRIAL

Uses: In any Industrial District as indicated on the Building Zoning Map, no building or premises shall be used and no building or part of a building shall be erected which is intended or designed to be used, except accessorily and incidentally, for any of the following purposes:

Explosives or fireworks manufacture.

And with that change the town had signaled its intention to mitigate the risk posed by the Napolitano brothers' pyrotechnics business. It seemed as it if was only a matter of time before the manufactories would be shut down.

But what if nature, saboteurs, or perhaps the brothers themselves beat them to the punch?

Four residents of Springfield, Massachusetts; Romeo Bernier of 48 Adams Street, Laurence Carbine of 47 Hebron Street, Ferdinand Ionini of 143 Union Street, and Albert Gaudrey of 22 Sterling Street, were hard at work in the Assembly Building at the Napolitano's fireworks factory on May 22, 1930.

The surrounding woods made for a quiet place to work, with the occasional sound of twittering birds providing nature's soothing soundtrack.

At 8:20, harshly interrupting the serene scene, the sound of three or four loud popping noises echoed inside the shack where the employees labored. The men froze, looked at each other immediately recognizing the reports, and bolted for the woods through the open building door.

There, about 50 feet behind them, a shed storing aerial bombs was on fire, launching rockets into the air and into the woods. Within seconds a second building, 40 feet away from the first, erupted, driving the retreating men to the ground from the concussive force. More rockets filled the air, some narrowly missing the men as they rose and began to run once more.

A third building exploded, and the frantic employees fell to the earth again. Wide-eyed they willed themselves to their feet and continued their flight towards safety.

All around them the sound of wailing rocketry filled the woods as well as the skies overhead. Projectiles screamed as they launched, some exploding above, others impacting trees, detonating on impact.

The woods were on fire.

As people began to arrive on the scene an oil tank near the main assembly building went up in smoke, spraying burning oil over Gaudery's automobile parked nearby and uninsured, setting it ablaze.

A fourth building, this one concrete, caught fire, its contents erupting as well.

At the farm of Addison Harvey Brainerd, less than a half-mile from the site, Agnes Mary Brainard, Addison's daughter, turned to see a pillar of flame and a huge black cloud roil skyward followed by an explosive force that shook the house.

Both Hartford and Rockville, each 15 miles away, residents reported hearing the incident as well.

Alerted to the blast by the eruption as well as from frantic calls from concerned residents, the North Thompsonville Fire Department, as it had at least twice before, responded to the site. The scene that met them this time though, resembled none of the previous events.

The Thompsonville Press

THE ONLY NEWSPAPER PUBLISHED IN THE TOWN OF ENFIELD, CONN.

FIFTY FIRST YEAR—No. 5.   THOMPSONVILLE, CONN., THURSDAY, MAY 22, 1930.   Subscription $2.50 Per Year—Single Copy 5c

ANNUAL POPPY SALE HERE NEXT SATURDAY

Yearly Effort to Raise Funds For Care of Disabled and Needy War Veterans Will Be Conducted by Legion Post.

Miss Griffin Honored At Pre-Nuptial Event

CARPET COMPANY TO CO-OPERATE IN CELEBRATION

Local Industry to Take An Active Part in the Plans For 250th Anniversary — Will Stress Industrial Importance

Fireworks Plant Wrecked By Terrific Blast This Morning

Four Men Narrowly Escape Death As Plant of New England Fireworks Company on Brainard Road Is Practically Demolished—Heard and Felt For Miles Around—Explosion Shook Buildings, Shattered Windows and Broke Crockery, But Damage Outside of Plant Is Small—One Employee Suffers From Shock—Cause of Explosion Is Unknown.

Town Will Play Host To Former Residents

Invitations Being Sent Out This Week to About 2000 Persons Who Were Born or For Some Period Resided Here, to Be Present at the 250th Anniversary Celebration Next June.

MEMORIAL DAY PLANS COMPLETE

Final Arrangements for the Exercises Made At a Meeting of Committee Last Evening.

An Invitation

Decision Gives Power Company Compensation

Utilities Power Project Would Be Reimbursed But Otherwise Compelled to Leave in Effect Its Present Diversion of Its Waters For Use of the Metropolitan District of Boston.

SAFETY MONTH IS NEARING VERY SUCCESSFUL END

No Mishaps So Far During May to Mar Intensive Effort Being Made Among the Employees of Carpet Plant.

FRANK BARBER IS SPEAKER AT ROTARY LUNCH

Analizes Part That Disposition Plays in Life Before Members of Local Club—Goody Goes to National Convention

Wreckage of Fireworks Shed Destroyed by Explosion

The woods were being scorched and the intense heat attempted to drive the firefighters back toward the road, but the men drove steadily forward, even as rockets continued to burst above and around them.

Employing a chemical tank specifically used for fighting forest fires, the men pushed onward, toward a standing building known to contain completed bombs, all the while keeping an eye and a steady stream of water pointed at a small red building which was well stocked with dynamite.

Fire Chief John Manning directed the firefighting efforts while Police Chief Clyde Harris and the men under his command managed the hundreds of cars attempting to view the conflagration.

Soon Pasquale and Saboto Napolitano arrived on the scene, making their way through the throng of people surrounding the site. The buildings that had held $15,000 ($270,000 in 2020) worth of finished fireworks to be used in an upcoming Fourth of July celebration had been vaporized. An additional $15,000 of raw materials dedicated to meeting other Independence Day contracts were lost as well.

One saving grace was that there had been no loss of life.

Due to the nature of the business, there had been no insurance carried on the buildings or content.

"I'm done with manufacturing" Pasquale was overheard to say.

There was no thought of rebuilding. [82]

---

[82] The Thompsonville Press. May 22, 1930 edition. Page 1.
Hartford Courant. May 23, 1930 edition. Page 24.
Meriden Daily Journal. May 22, 1930 edition. Page 1.
New Britain Herald. May 22, 1932 edition. Page 1 & 2.

CODE AUTHORITY BOARD OF THE PYROTECHNIC
MANUFACTURING INDUSTRY
MILLS BUILDING
WASHINGTON, D. C.

OFFICE OF THE
EXECUTIVE SECRETARY

December 18, 1934.

New England Fireworks Mfg. & Display Co.,
524 Union Street,
Springfield, Mass.

Dear Sirs:

This will acknowledge receipt of your
notation on our letter of December 4th, in which
you advise us that your Company has been out of
business since 1929.

Assuming this statement to be true, it
would, of course, be unnecessary for you to file
any reports with this Administration.

Very truly yours,

Executive Secretary.

Just as had been done with their Boston namesake *The New England Fireworks Company,* the committee on Mercantile Affairs of the Commonwealth of Massachusetts, by way of House Bill 1275, legally dissolved the *New England Fireworks Manufacturing and Display Company* of Springfield, Massachusetts, on March 15, 1932.

Years later in response to the Code Authority Board of the Pyrotechnic Manufacturing Industry, Pasquale claimed that the business had dissolved in 1929. Perhaps it was just an attempt to dissuade the pyrotechnic group from further contacting him.

Or perhaps there was a bit of truth to the response – not insofar as the termination date, but to the fact that the manufacturing of pyrotechnics had been stopped.

Then again, if manufacturing had indeed been halted, why would Napolitano still be purchasing pyrotechnic supplies from C. W. Campbell Company of New York? And not in small quantities either, as suggested by the February 6, 1933, receipt displayed on the next page.

This was **four** years after Napolitano claimed the company had dissolved, and **three** years after the explosion that had in effect shut down the business.

The timing was off.

Six months before responding to the Code Authority, and once again **four** years after claiming the company was no longer in the manufacturing business, the Fireworks King was interviewed in a July 1, 1934, Springfield Republican article reflecting on what made a good pyrotechnics display.

Of curious interest was that the story mentioned that Pasquale had "dabbled in fireworks for 18 years", which would have preceded the founding of his company by nine years. That would have put Patsy at 17 years of age, the same time when he was working as a Soda Clerk for the Louis Kroh Liggett Company. Somehow it is difficult to equate the skills of mixing an ice cream soda with the expertise required to mix combustible solid rocket fuel and explosives.

Based on the article though, one could not question his understanding of the fireworks arts, and what was required to put on a first-class aerial display.

The demise of his manufacturing company, whatever the true year, could not subdue Napolitano's love of fireworks, and, although he seemingly no longer produced explosives himself, he still commanded the rockets, cannons, and bombs, and conducted their performance.

He would do so once again at the Eastern States Exposition in Massachusetts, just three days after the projected publish date of the news article.

Perhaps he would launch his signature displays such as "The Acrobatic Monkey", "The Dancing Bear", "The Ferris Wheel", "A Man Milking a Cow", or the crowd pleasing "The Trained Pigs on a See-Saw".

At the celebration Patsy would be in his element, freed from the overwhelming stresses of manufacturing; simply choreographing an aerial display to please hundreds, if not thousands of enraptured fans.

Two years later, unlike his fireworks, the showman, the Fireworks King, Pasquale Napolitano, quietly passed away at Wesson Memorial Hospital in Springfield, Massachusetts at the young age of 37.

The King was dead.

Long Live the King.

As an extra bonus for those who read Italian I have included on the next two pages a letter from Felippo Benciovegna of the Imperial Fireworks Company of America to Pasquale Napolitano. The letter is dated a few weeks after the Thompsonville factory explosion and I assume it refers to the tragedy.

Buona fortuna leggendo questo.

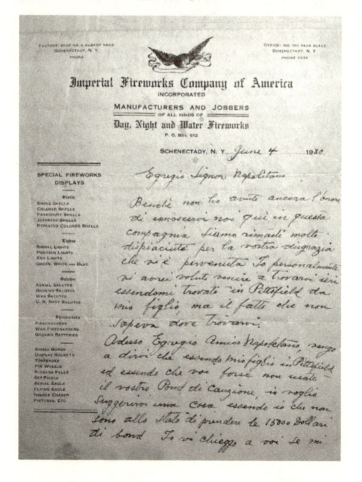

The second page of the letter.

*vorreste fare usare il vostro Bond e prenni
qualche piu o meno potesse venire in accordo.
Io posso prendere 4 o 5 feste Americane e 2 o 3
Italiane potete lavorare voi ed io.
Massimiano e ritornato in Pittsfield molto ammalato
e quasi inabile al lavoro e la sua disgrazia
mi dispiace altrettanto e non mai cercherò di
li levargli qualche festa se lui e abile a parla
Cosicche non voglio costringermi a prendere
il Bond e perciò mi dirigo da voi e metterò
in accordo, e se voi avete molte feste da
fare, potete venire libberamente in Schenectady
e farmi qualche si serve colle vostre mani
nella mia fattoria
Attendo una vostra risposta o potete venire
a trovarmi alla sopraddetta direzione
Vi Saluto e non pensate a niente
Vostro Amico
Filippo Bencivenga
100 Park Place
Schenectady N.Y.*

5: STOP THIEF

*Now there is a little thing I want to mention to you -
just quietly and under the cover - I hope the Enfield
Society for the Detection of Horse Thieves and
Robbers is still in operation. I know the Society was
keeping up its headquarters in Enfield a few years
ago. And I hope the Society is all set for some
emergencies — just in case something happens next
November that we don't expect. Because now I am
going to give you some quotations — now these are
not my remarks at all, these are quotes — because if
the Republicans should win this election, the
society is going to have lots of business after November
the 4th.[83]*

The word constable comes from the French conestable,
which originally was defined as a person holding a public
office but further evolved to mean a person exercising a

---

[83] THOMPSONVILLE, CONNECTICUT (Rear platform train, 2:03
p.m.) Harry S. Truman remarks October 6, 1952.

higher form of authority (connétable).

In England, before the colonies had been established, public civil officers, or constables (unpaid), maintained the peace within an assigned district.

The English constable was originally a post in the Royal Court; but the role later evolved into a local office, subordinate to a sheriff or mayor. Despite the official designation, the investigation and prosecution of crimes remained a private matter to be handled by the victims.

From the early 16th to the early 19th century, English merchants, traders, church members, insurers, and others employed private individuals to protect their property and their persons. Protection became a commodity, available to anyone who could afford it. Those without the money to directly pay for recovery services offered rewards instead.

The process in many ways resembled bounty hunting.

Soon entire British communities began paying private citizens for the capture and conviction of thieves, and a standard set of fees was established to add some structure to the system. Any citizen, not only constables, could earn money by pursuing and capturing thieves and robbers.

As translated by the American colonies, the constable was essentially the first law enforcement officer. His duties varied from managing and monitoring sealed weights and measures, surveying land, announcing marriages, executing all warrants, collecting taxes, meeting out punishment when necessary, and generally enforcing the peace.

In the late 1770s and early 1800s crime in North Central Connecticut wasn't as much of a concern as basic survival was the focus for both businesses and families.

Constables were assigned by the individual towns and a fee structure was set in place for certain offences, such as 67 cents for attending a trial or 9 cents for serving a summons.

An Act regulating Fees in certain cases and for other purposes.

§ 1. **B**E it enacted by the Governour and Council and House of Representatives in General Court assembled, That the fees allowed to sheriffs, constables and other persons, for the service of writs and processes, and for other services, in cases hereinafter specified, shall be as follows, viz. For each mile travel *five cents,* to be computed from the place of the officers abode, to the place of service, and from thence to the place of return; also for travel across any toll bridge or ferry actually passed, in making the service of a writ or execution, the sum by law payable at such bridge or ferry, for man and horse, if actually paid on the service or return of such writ or execution, but not any sum for passing a turnpike gate.

For serving every summons by reading $0 9
For - - - by copy 0 12
For - attachment by reading or copy 0 12
For taking bail and bail bond on each writ of attachment, if returnable before a Justice of Peace, 0 24
If returnable to the city or county court and the demand therein be five hundred dollars or under, 0 50
If the demand be more than five hundred dollars, 1 0

And in all cases except in writs and declarations on promissory note and book debt, according to the forms prescribed by statute when necessarily served by copy, and the copy exclusive of the endorsement shall make a page of twenty eight lines ten words in a line for each copy 0 25
And for each endorsement of service that shall make fourteen lines ten words in a line, 0 12½
And for every additional page or part of a page of such copy or endorsement at the same rate; and for a copy of the endorsement when necessary to be made, and it shall make half a page as aforesaid or more, at the same rate.

§ 2. Be it further enacted, That in all cases in which any claim shall be made for any compensation to any person on the service of an attachment or execution for time, and expenses, in keeping, securing or removing property taken thereon, the person who served such attachment or execution shall make out his bill on the same for such compensation, specifying the items therein, viz. the labour done and by whom, the time spent, and how long, the money paid (if any) and to whom, and for what; and in case of attachment, the court in which the bill of cost shall finally be taxed, may on consideration, allow therefor such sum as is just and reasonable, and the same shall be added to and taxed with the cost in the action.

§ 3. Be it further enacted, That for levying and collecting every execution when the money is actually collected and paid over, or where the debt is secured and satisfied by the officer to the acceptance of the creditor, where the amount of the execution does not exceed three dollars and thirty four cents, the officer collecting the same shall be allowed seventeen cents, and two cents on each dollar on the amount of the execution that exceeds that sum; and where the execution is levied on the body of the debtor, and he is committed to gaol, one cent on the dollar on the amount of the execution shall be allowed to the officer and no more, any law, usage or custom to the contrary notwithstanding.

§ 4. Be it further enacted, That a sheriff, deputy sheriff or constable shall be allowed the sum of sixty seven cents for attending the trial of an action before a justices court when he shall attend and the same is necessary; a sheriff for attending the general assembly, superior or county court for each day he shall actually attend, the sum of two dollars and fifty cents, in full of all services and expenses; a deputy-sheriff or constable, for the like services the sum of two dollars; the general sheriffs in this state for distributing the public laws and proclamations, and for their actual attendance on the general assembly at election each the sum of twelve dollars.

§ 5. Be it further enacted, That sheriffs and constables for committing any person to gaol on mesne or final process shall be allowed twenty cents per mile for travel from the place of arrest to the gaol in lieu of all other expenses.

§ 6. Be it further enacted, That no sheriff, constable or other officers shall add or make any other items of fees, not specified in this act, for the service or return of any civil process whatever, nor for any other purpose in civil cases, but shall be wholly confined to the fees in this act specified.

§ 7. Be it further enacted, That whenever a sheriff, deputy-sheriff, or constable, shall have received the money on any execution in his hands for collection, and the same shall have been demanded of him by any person authorized to receive the same, and such officer shall neglect or refuse to pay the same on such demand, he shall pay, and the person entitled to the money shall have a right to recover and receive of such officer, two per cent. a month, on the amount so received, from the time of such demand, until the same be paid.

§ 8. Be it further enacted, That every sheriff shall have a right to demand and receive of every deputy appointed, or to be appointed, for the hazard and risque of such appointment, a sum not exceeding forty dollars annually, and in the same proportion for any less term than one year; which sum shall be in full of all claims and demands on such deputy for and on account of such appointment, except when the sheriff may be sued on account of the default of such deputy, in which case the sheriff shall have a right to demand and receive on the bond of such deputy the sum of seven dollars in addition to such sum or sums which may be recovered of the sheriff or which he may have to pay on account of the default of such deputy. And no sheriff shall, directly or indirectly take or receive of any gaoler any sum whatever, as fee or reward for his appointment, or for continuing him in office. And no sheriff shall, directly or indirectly, take or receive any other or greater compensation from any deputy by him appointed, than what is provided for in this act. And if any sheriff shall, contrary to the provisions of this act, demand, take or receive any sum, or other compensation, of any gaoler or deputy-sheriff, on such fact being made to appear before any county or superior court, such sheriff shall forever thereafter be incapable of holding the office of sheriff in this State.

§ 9 Be it further enacted, That if upon complaint made to the Governour and Council, it shall appear that any sheriff illegally detains after demand, any money by him collected on any execution: or that any sheriff, without any just or legal cause, neglects or refuses to satisfy any execution, issued against him within the life thereof, such sheriff shall be declared incapable of any longer holding the office of sheriff in this State, and shall be removed accordingly.

§ 10. Be it further enacted, That the act, entitled "An Act for regulating fees in certain cases," and also "An Act to regulate the office of Sheriff," passed in May 1815, and also that part of the act entitled "An Act for regulating Salaries and Fees," so far as regards the sheriffs' and constables' fees, on civil process, and also "An Act in addition to an Act entitled an Act in alteration of an Act, entitled an Act regulating Salaries and Fees," passed in May 1808, be and the same are hereby repealed.

Genera. Assembly, October Session, 1816.
CHARLES DENISON, Speaker
of the House of Representatives.
JOHN COTTON SMITH, Governour.
Attest. THOMAS DAY, Secretary.

Crimes were rare and responsibility difficult to deny as most everyone in town knew everyone else, news traveled fast, and secrets difficult to keep. When crime did visit itself upon the community it was more than likely to come from outside the town.

Like when a horse was stolen.

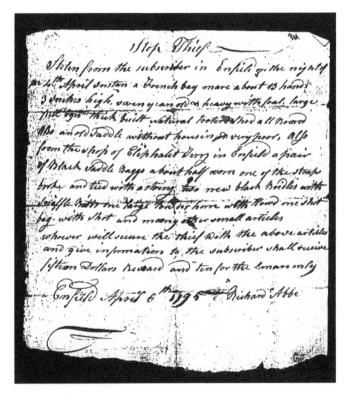

In 1795 Richard Abbe and Eliphalet Terry posted a reward of 15 dollars for information on a stolen horse, saddle bags, bridles, powder horns, powder, shirts, and other unnamed articles.

During the late 1700s and early 1800s regional papers such as the Connecticut Courant, Connecticut Mirror, and Springfield Republican, and were rife with announcements of stolen horses, runaway servants, and petty crimes which would have fallen under the purview of local constables.

Constables, the world's first private police force, were more apt to pursue "low hanging fruit" such as arresting trespassers or drunks to increase their pay. Pursuing horse thieves was a more costly challenge with less chance for success.

This is borne out by the posting of a 15-dollar reward by Richard Abbe and Eliphalet Terry in 1795 for information on, or the capture of, the individual or individuals who had stolen Abbe's horse and other items of Terry's. It is unknown whether the reward bore fruit.

The lack of attention by local constables to the plight of the unique challenges faced by the farmers prompted certain concerned residents of the towns of Enfield and Warehouse Point to band together to form a protective group they called *The Enfield and Warehouse Point Society for Detecting Thieves, Robbers, &c* in 1796.

Protective, or vigilante, groups weren't that unique when specific issues were required to be addressed that weren't getting attention from the law. Some of these concerns were very specific such as when protective groups were formed like the Worcester Association for the Protection of Fruit[84] or the Connecticut Society for the Suppression of Vice and the Promotion of Good Morals. [85]

Large organizations weren't excluded from creating protective societies to address pressing issues, such as when the Indiana Bankers Association formed the Indiana Bankers Vigilante Organization whose job it was to provide protection for the expanding bank infrastructure in that

---

[84] American Antiquarian Society, Worcester, Massachusetts
[85] Fraser, Pedagogue for God's Kingdom: Lyman Beecher and the Second Great Awakening pgs 17,19

state against masked robbers.

Members of the Indiana Bankers Vigilante Organization gathered together for their "Second Annual Shoot" picnic

Although the founding articles of *The Enfield and Warehouse Point Society for Detecting Thieves, Robbers, &c* have yet to be located, a partial list of the key members can be gleaned from meeting announcements published over the early 1800s.

- William Dixon (Enfield Resident/Attorney)
- Daniel Abbe, Jr. (Enfield Resident/Innholder)
- Peter R. Field (Enfield Resident/Innholder)
- Daniel Bartlett, Jr. (Warehouse Point Innholder)
- John Olmsted (Enfield Resident/Merchant)
- Luther Parsons (Enfield Resident/Merchant)
- Eliphalet Terry (Enfield Resident)
- Henry Terry (Enfield Resident)

Most of the members mentioned in the announcements were residents of Enfield. Due to the importance of Warehouse Point as a port to the region, it was a natural fit for the two towns to ally in addressing those types of crimes that might otherwise escape the attention of the constables.

The year this society was formed is recorded in one

article as 1796,[86] although the first published announcement of annual meetings can only be found in newspapers as far back as 1812.[87]

The 1796 date is additionally supported by the 1795 reward posting/letter of Enfield farmers/residents Richard Abbe and Eliphalet Terry [shown in the previous graphic[88]].

In 1801, Eliphalet Terry and Henry Terry of Enfield, Connecticut, submitted a petition to the Connecticut General Assembly asking that their protective society be sanctioned by the state, having been in established in 1796.[89] This would support the assumption that these two men were members of the *Enfield and Warehouse Point Society for Detecting Thieves, Robbers, &c* group and would further support the establishment date of that society as 1796.

The 1801 petition of the Terry brothers was denied by the state legislature, with no reason cited, and the following is the transcription of that document:

To the Honorable General Assembly now in session.

The petition of Eliphalet Terry and Henry Terry both of Enfield in Hartford County, humbly showeth that they, with their officiates, in the year 1796, formed themselves into a society for the purpose of Detecting Thieves, Robbers and Felons of every description and have contributed a considerable sum to remain as a fund for carrying their purpose into effect.

And your Petitioners represent that nor being able to

---

[86] Ann-Marie Szymanski. The New England Quarterly, Vol. 78, No. 3 (Sep., 2005), pp. 407-439 (33 pages)

[87] Connecticut Mirror, December 14, 1812.

[88] Letter is property of H. Pierson Hammond of West Hartford. Original photostat CT State Library Sept 18, 1935.

[89] Connecticut Archival Record (Corporations) II:79

carry into effect such beneficial regulations as the majority of the society are desirous of adopting and having a method of perpetuating their fund, they are apprehensive of possibly failing to effect the object of their association without the interposition of your Honors.

They therefore pray the legislature to take their case into their wise consideration and grant them an Act of Incorporation by the name of the "Enfield Society for Detecting Thieves Robbers and Felons of every description" with powers of making bye laws and regulations as to your Honors shall [indecipherable] prosper –

Provided always that the funds of [the] society shall not exceed the sum of one thousand dollars and they in duty bound shall ever pray.

Dated at Enfield
May 19, 1801
Eliphalet Terry
Henry Terry

Based on the shared year of their founding, 1796, we can safely assume that these two organizations were one and the same, despite their different names. Henry Terry is never mentioned in the meeting announcements for the combined society but does appear on the 1823-member list of The Enfield Society for the Detection of Thieves and Robbers. Eliphalet Terry does not, but he died in 1810 so that clears up any mystery there.

The Red Hook Society for the Apprehension and Detention of Horse Thieves [Red Hook, New York] claims to be the oldest horse thief apprehension society in the United States, as it was founded on October 28, 1796.

In 2021 the Red Hook Society demanded that the *Dedham Massachusetts Society for Apprehending Horse Thieves* stop claiming that they were the oldest such organization in the nation, which was the claim of the Red Hook association.

Dedham relented.

The month *The Enfield and Warehouse Point Society for Detecting Thieves, Robbers, &c* was founded is yet unknown, but if that month or day was earlier than that of Red Hook, and if those documents identify the society as being established to address horse thievery, then Red Hook's designation as the country's oldest protective society may be challenged by Enfield as well.

The focus on horse stealing would be a requirement to make a claim to be the first society *of its kind* as Northampton, Massachusetts, had founded the *Northampton Society for the Detection of Thieves and Robbers* in 1782. This would establish them as the *first true generalized protective society*, but since they ceased to exist by 1881, they cannot claim to be the longest continually operating.

Next in line for consideration would be the *Woodstock* [Connecticut] *Theft Detecting Society*, founded in 1793, which, because they don't specify a specific crime, might claim the crown of being the first formed to fight crime in general, predating the assumed Enfield 1796 date.

Claiming to be first can be full of caveats.

Each year, like clockwork, *The Enfield and Warehouse Point Society* posted an announcement for their annual gathering where outstanding business for the group would be discussed, or officers voted in.

THE members of the Enfield and Warehouse Point society for detecting Thieves, Robbers, &c. are hereby notified that their annual meeting will be holden at the dwelling-house of Peter R. Field, innholder in said Enfield on the 12th day of December next, at 6 o'clock in the afternoon.   By Order of Committee,
WM. DIXON, Clerk.
Enfield, Nov. 10, 1814.   2w 1

By 1822 though, there was a noticeable change in the language of the announcement.

"THE Enfield and Warehouse Point Society for detecting Thieves, Robbers," &c. are hereby notified that their annual meeting will be holden at Mr. Peter R. Fields' Inn in Enfield, on Monday the 13th day of January next, at four o'clock P. M.—At which time, will be tried the deferred motion, for withdrawing a part of the funds of said society—Also, a complete list of the members as transferred, &c. will be presented.
Per Order,   LUTHER PARSONS, Clerk.
Enfield, Dec. 6, 1822.   20

For an unstated reason, funds were being proposed to be withdrawn, and *a complete list of the members as transferred, etc, will be presented* (see previous advertisement).

The following year there was no announcement in the local papers for the expected annual meeting of *The Enfield and Warehouse Point Society*, confirming it was disbanded.

A document does exist that announces the adoption of the founding constitution by *The Enfield Society for the Detection of Thieves and Robbers* on January 30, 1823. The full list of members who signed on follows[90] (bold italicized are members of The Enfield and Warehouse Point Society, while bold asterisked identifies petitioners for the Enfield Society for Detecting Thieves Robbers and Felons of every description) [91]:

Henry Terry*
William Dixon
L.T. Pease
Lot Killam
Peter Reynolds
Joseph Olmsted
Heber Pease
Timothy Killam
Daniel Abbe
Levi Abbe
John King
Fletcher Prudden
Sylvester Lusk
Thomas Knight
Walter Collins
Horace Medcalf
Simon Olmsted
Timothy Abbe
Mathew Thompson
John Olmsted
Solomon Terry
Ephraim Prudden
Orrin Thompson

Henry Kingsbury
George Meacham
Harris Meacham
Selah Terry
Daniel Gowdy
Hill Gowdy
Robert Gowdy
Ebenesor Chapin
David Gates
Geer Terry
Christopher H. Terry
Jabez Collins
Horace Pease
Reuben Pease
George Allen
William Adams
John Bartlett, Jr.
Henry Thompson
Samuel Booth
Elisha Parsons
Samuel A. Stillman
Isaac Wright
John Burbank

The following is a general assumption I have made based on information recovered.

---

[90] Challenge of Change p 173
[91] Point of Interest Eliphalet Terry (senior) had died in 1810

In 1796 a society was formed to address crimes that residents of both Enfield and Warehouse Point were experiencing. These were challenges that local constables were unable or unwilling to address.

In 1801 this same society petitioned the General Assembly for formal recognition by the state as an incorporated entity.

The state denied their petition for an unknown reason.

The Society continued their mission as defined at their founding until 1823 when they splintered, and the Enfield group was renamed with a new set of Articles to define them.

The Warehouse Point group retained the original name, as newspaper posts continued announcing annual meetings for *The Warehouse Point Society for Detecting Thieves, Robbers, &c.*

NOTICE.

THE members of the Warehouse Point Society for detecting Thieves, Robbers, &c. are hereby notified that their annual meeting will be held at John A. Chase's Inn, at Warehouse Point, on the 2d Monday of January next, at 6 o'clock P. M. to elect officers for the year ensuing, and to transact any other business proper to be done at said meeting.

Per order of the Committee,

HARVEY HOLKINS, Secretary.

East-Windsor, Dec. 31, 1836.   2w

The East Windsor Society for Detecting Thieves and Robbers traces its roots back to 1841 when 29 resident vigilantes assembled in the home of Jonah Griswold to organize the town's volunteer society. [92] Whether this

---

[92] Hartford Courant, January 11, 2000, *A Group On The Lookout For New Blood*

society was simply a renaming, or reconstitution of The Warehouse Point Society is unclear, but, as Warehouse Point is a village within the borders of East Windsor it would seem likely.

The first recorded challenge answered by the 1823 *Enfield Society for the Detection of Thieves and Robbers* wasn't until 1842, when Levi Abbe called out the pursuers to recover his horses which he believed had been stolen by persons unknown.

At their next annual meeting the group recorded the results of that pursuit where it was noted that the horses had not been stolen but had merely wandered off. As a result, Rufus Parson, who was not a founding member, made a motion that the Society pay the expenses of all of the pursuers who had engaged in the search for the Abbe's horses, except for costs incurred by the steed's owner – Levi Abbe.

The motion was passed.

Records indicate five more pursuits from 1843 through 1862, one of which was yet another request for assistance from Mr. Abbe. This time, in 1851, his horse actually was stolen, and a recovery expense of $50 was recorded.

In 1854 the Society responded once again, not to a stolen horse event but to a reported break-in at the home of Augustus G. Hazard. The assistance must have been successful as a fee was paid to Colonel Robert Abbe of $17.50 for his successful pursuit services. Hazard must have been a member of the Society at that time as the protective group only answered the call of its membership – a benefit of joining the exclusive club.

Lifetime membership dues began as one dollar and

remain so to the time of this writing. Of course, that 1823 $1 fee equates to $28 [2020], so the cost of joining the Society has steadily gone down over the years, more so when you consider the fee as a percent of yearly earnings.

ENFIELD.

The town authorities met on Monday and elected the forty jurymen required by law, appointed the selectmen, a special board of health, and ate the annual town dinner. On the same day there was a meeting of the society for detecting thieves and robbers, and the old officers were reëlected for the ensuing year, and a dividend of five dollars to each member was declared, payable after the 10th day of January, the funds of the society having risen to more than one thousand dollars out of the fee of one dollar each member has to pay when he joins and the interest accrued on the investments.

In the early years of the Society members could borrow from the group's treasury based solely on a personal note, as there was not only a level of trust between members, but a realization justice would be swift if the note remained unpaid.

In the late 1880's the Society even began to pay a dividend, of varying amounts, to members. One year the dividend was five times the initiation amount, or about $144 in 2020. It is unclear how many years that dividend was paid out.

An interesting story about the Society was recounted in a Hartford Courant article in 1933.

An unnamed member of the group had a valuable antique stolen from his house. After a week had passed the

141

member contacted *The Enfield Society for the Detection of Thieves and Robbers* to request their assistance in recovering the item.

His request was reportedly laughed off with a derisive response of "Why don't you go to the police?"

The member retorted "There's no need for that. What's this Society for anyway?"

Chagrined, a sympathetic member took out an advertisement in a local paper describing the crime as well as the item.

Another member, unnamed again, who had moved away from the area yet still received the local publication, read the article, and set out in search of the antique.

In due time his determination was rewarded as he located the item in a dingy shop in Boston, Massachusetts, 85 miles away. The antique was recovered, possibly making this the furthest *The Enfield Society* has ever imposed its anti-crime influence.

By the turn of the following century, the Enfield police department was established in 1903, with Edward Bromage, a former town constable, inserted as the first Chief of Police. There was one fulltime patrolman under his direction at the time, with other part time officers able to be called upon should the need arise.

The move to a fulltime police force made economic sense as the local constabulary was becoming too expensive.

By 1906 the new lawman of the town had begun to exert his control over areas not previously addressed by the Society. As reported in The Meriden Daily Journal:

> *Bromage, chief of Enfield's police, made a wild west entrance upon a prizefight in R. A. Griese's hotel in*

Hazardville last night and translated most of a lively prizefight to the Thompsonville jail.

The principals were "Young Jones" of New York and "Bill Green" of Buffalo. Later they gave their names for station house purposes as William Clark of Northampton, and Marry Larkin of this city [Springfield, MA]. The latter are supposed to be true.

Their agreement to meet at Hazardville had been heralded among the "sports" of Springfield and the suburbs, and a choice crowd went down to see the battle. The mill took place in a little hall on the second floor of the hotel.

The next year a December 14th Hartford Courant article presented a more pedestrian example of crime and reward.

Chief Bromage had secured evidence used in apprehending and convicting Thomas Burke of Enfield for the crime of stealing chickens.

Due to his history as a constable, Bromage petitioned the court to collect the reward due to the person responsible for capturing the chicken thief.

Judge Wheeler denied the request as the Chief was a paid officer of the Town of Enfield.

Perhaps Bromage should have called in pursuers from *The Enfield Society for the Detection of Thieves and Robbers* to handle the crime.

.

6: SEXING CHICKENS

In July of 1957 the case of the Inter-Maritime Forwarding Company, Incorporated versus the United States was heard in Federal Customs Court. At the heart of the matter was the taxing of a device known as the "Keeler Chixexers" or "Chixexer Tubes," apparatus which was used to help determine the sex of day-old chicks.

One witness for the plaintiff stated that:

> *...the use of an instrument, such as plaintiff's exhibit 1, in the sexing of chicks has the advantage over that of the so-called "cloacal" or manual method, inasmuch as the imported device magnifies, whereas the latter operation requires keen eyesight to disclose the sex organ.*[93]

A witness for the defendant was George Okazaki, an assistant general manager with the American Chick Sexing Association, which furnished chick-sexing services to hatcherymen throughout the United States. His duties included supervision of over 300 chick sexers and the direction of the company chick-sexing school, in which he

---

[93] Inter-Maritime Forwarding Co. v. United States, 1957

also taught. The witness had, since 1933, personally sexed from four to five million chicks for breeders all over the United States.

Inter-Maritime lost the suit, the court maintaining that the equipment in question was optical in nature and not agricultural, and thus subject to a much higher import duty.

The skill of sexing though, was clearly an established need in the trade in the late 1950s.

In 1925 an article on differentiating the sexes of living baby chicks appeared in the *Japan Journal of Zoological Science.* It was written by scientists Kiyoshi Masui and Juro Hashimoto of the Tokyo Imperial University.

A GUIDE TO SEXING CHICKS

CHARLES S. GIBBS

References to the publication and those responsible were made in two separate instances, one in the book *A Guide To Sexing Chicks* and the other a journal article Sexing Baby Chicks by the same author Charles S. Gibbs, an employee at the Massachusetts Agricultural Experimental Station which was within the Massachusetts State College [later called the University of Massachusetts] in Amherst, Mass.

In the November 30, 1933, Annual Report for the same

institution Gibbs reported:

> *A demonstration of sexing living baby chicks was put on at the Poultry Breeders' School this year (1933). Considerable interest was shown, and the method may find some practical use in New England. Schools are being established on the Pacific Coast and in the Middle West for the determination of sex in living baby chicks, and New England poultrymen may be forced to sex their chicks in the future in order to hold their trade.*[94]

Based on the success of the presentation, a laboratory for sexing chickens was set up at the same school which would accommodate a class of up to ten students. Upon completion of the facility notifications were sent out to agents in the surrounding counties to identify, and make aware of the educational opportunity, appropriate poultrymen, or their employees, who were interested in acquiring the knowledge and skills required in "sexing" chickens. There were projected to be two instructional lessons provided to the trainees, with a predictive accuracy expected of between 80-90% after the first lesson.

As Gibbs stated in his article:

> *Skill is developed only by practice. A persistent student will see the process and its relation to the folds more clearly as he labors from day to day. Gradually he will be able to differentiate one type from another and to determine sex with ease. Skill in sexing baby chicks can be acquired by anybody possessing patience, agility, and good sight, as is being demonstrated in*

---

[94] Massachusetts Agricultural Experiment Station, Amherst – Annual report, 1934, pg 59.

Massachusetts.[95]

Chester Pilch was born to Joseph and Karolina Pilch of Feeding Hills, a village within Agawam, Massachusetts, in 1912. Fourteen months later he was joined by brother Francis. The Polish family would remain at two children until eleven years later when brother Edward arrived.

The boy's father was a simple man, who claimed to be an experienced carpenter as well as a jack-of-all-trades. Joseph lacked drive and focus, but the family succeeded well enough despite his shortcomings. Fruit trees, a garden, and a small flock of chickens provided food as well as produce to sell to neighbors to supplement the family's ebb and flow income.

Chester and Francis couldn't have been more different.

Chester was relatively unpolished, a mirror of his father, while Francis was studious, intelligent, and seemingly primed for a life beyond working the earth.

—POULTRY—

New Britain Poultry Association Meeting Monday Evening
Nov. 3, 8 P. M.. I. O. O. F. Hall, Arch St.
OPEN MEETING
Everyone interested in Poultry Keeping invited to attend.
Prof. W. F. Kirkpatrick to speak relating to his trip in
Europe, also showing pictures of the poultry
exhibition at Barcelona, Spain
Refreshments to be served

But Joseph's first-born seemed to have the drive his father lacked. In high school he joined a local chapter of the

---

[95] Gibbs. Sexing Baby Chicks. Pg 208.

4-H organization which was committed to encouraging both boys and girls to get involved in "working the land".

Surely the 1924 World Exhibition of Poultry in Barcelona, Spain must have caught the boy's attention as it was the first time American fowlers would participate in the event, and the 4-H would have played up the occasion. As reported in the April 6th edition of the Hartford Courant, fully twenty-five percent of the poultry participants would come from the Nutmeg State. White Leghorns, Rhode Island Reds, and White Plymouth Rocks, among other less recognizable hen species, would well represent the New England region.

Regional Shows like those at the Eastern States Exposition in Springfield, Massachusetts and the New England Poultry Show held in Hartford, Connecticut, mirrored the enthusiasm of the global events drawing competitors and suppliers in hopes of fame and fortune.

Of particular interest at the 1931 poultry show held at the Calvary Armory in West Hartford was an electric incubator capable of hatching up to 40,000 chicks, separated on individual trays. Surprisingly the original design for the electric incubator had been filed thirty-one years earlier by Granville T. Woods of Columbus, Ohio, known at the time as the "Black Edison".[96]

Chester had graduated high school in 1931, while the country was gripped in the beginnings of the Great Depression, and he was turned down at each attempt at gaining employment. Recalling his success during his high school 4-H years when he had purchased 200 chicks and had raised them, ultimately selling them for a profit, he refocused to his roots, acquiring 500 purebred Rhode Island Reds which he began to raise on his family farm.

In the Fall of 1933 heard of a unique educational

---

[96] Patent US1801300A (1900 granted / 1917 expired)

opportunity at the nearby Massachusetts State College centered on the art of sexing day old chicks. Intrigued the young man applied and was accepted into the program, no doubt his association with the 4-H helped him gain entrance. Taught by Professor Charles S. Gibbs, the work built on earlier research by the Chinese which had been enhanced and perfected in Japan.

Gibbs severely undershot the time required for students to reach peak proficiency, but within three years Chester had become a skilled master, earning a reputation throughout the Northeast while working on his own brood.

Sensing he was on the verge of greatness, Chester purchased the "Moody Road farm" in Enfield, Connecticut, in 1937 moving there with his brother Frances.

By 1938 the Hartford Courant printed an exclusive on the skilled 26-year-old young man. Seven years out of high school, with the country nearing the end of the Great Depression, Chester Pilch was employing his talents sexing chicks for area breeders at the tune of one hundred and twenty dollars per day (about $2,600 in 2020 dollars). By all standards Pilch was well on his way to becoming a wealthy man.

The newspaper continued:

> *He will get a call from a poultryman, set off at midnight to drive across the state, arrive at 3 a.m., put up his stand and sex chicks for six hours at a stretch so that a shipment can be made on a 10 o'clock morning for far away Delaware where the broilermen raise flocks of 100,000 at a profit and like to get New England stock.*
>
> *Between times Pilch keeps things going at his own hatcheries, where he gives employment to seven, including a steady job for his father and younger*

brother. His two 30,000-egg incubators cost $2500 each, and he has a total stock of about 10,000 head, layers, and young pullets. He has an average hatch of 10,000 chicks a week since January 1st of this year, and demand for them exceeds supply. He was financed with loans from banks prepared to extend credit to approved 4-H members.

By January of 1940 Pilch was advertising his own sexing school in the American Agriculturist, built on both his name and reputation.

Join Chet's Chick Sexing School and Service.

Learn with New England's pioneer sexer.

Over 1 million chicks separated in 7 years. Continuous classes. Most students attain over 90% accuracy in one week. Successful students throughout New England. Further details on request.

Hatcherymen: Write or phone your needs for commercial sexers. Phone Springfield, (Mass.) 4-0162.

Chester Pilch, Feeding Hills, Mass.

The purchased Moody Road Farm continued to expand, with the installation of new specialized buildings and offices. Chester set up a store at the site to sell prepared broilers as he began to breed chickens for rapid weight gain. His breeding program was so successful that his "genetically refined" chickens could be brought to market quicker than his competitors, allowing him to increase profits without increasing flock size or costs. His new breed quickly found purchasers all over the world and was marketed under the name *Cheterosis.*

POULTRY AND SUPPLIES 49

CHETEROSIS QUALITY SEXED CHICKS—Day old cockerels and pullets. Started chicks. New 1939 prices. Chester Pilch. Hazardville, Conn. Tel Thompsonville 3726

Unknown was whether Chester employed some of the tactics developed by Dr. Hubert Goodale who was, for a time, a research investigator at the same institution where Pilch had learned the art of sexing chicks. Goodale's concept of a "closed flock system" which he refined at the Massachusetts Experimental Station, resulted in an increase in chicken egg production of 200%. Given Chester's interest in improving yields and profits it's safe to assume he would have been intrigued enough to adopt the requisite practices.

As World War Two ended Chester continued to grow his establishment, opening a retail store on the Moody premises selling dressed chickens, eggs, turkeys, and capons. In a tip-of-the-cap to his earlier success, Chester opened the *Pilch School of Chick Sexing* which was approved for new students under the G. I. Bill. At the time there were less than one thousand chick sexors for the entirety of the United States, which meant that it was a wide-open field for a practiced examiner. The three-week sexing course attracted students from all over the world.

In 1949, much like the year before, Mother Nature dealt the poultry agency a blow as July temperatures topped one hundred degrees and a drought gripped the state. Egg production dropped off by thirty percent as hens slowed down their eating. Chickens can handle two to three days of above average temperature in a row, but an extended heat wave results in a noticeable reduction in egg production.

One year prior, in August of 1948, as temperatures soared, and remained high for weeks, Connecticut poultry died off by the thousands, and farmers learned valuable lessons in how to save their flocks. Poultrymen began systematic soaking of both their birds and coups to lower the core temperatures of the chickens as well as their environments.

Trouble arose as well in transporting birds as chicks older than three days were more likely to die during shipment. Before chicks reach three days old, they subsist without feeding, living on the remaining egg yolk within their tiny bodies. After three days though the birds must eat, and the collective body heat generated by consuming food raises the temperature in shipping crates, suffocating the birds.

Thankfully, after two weeks, the weather broke, and production slowly returned to normal.

July of 1951 offered a summer reminiscent of 1949, with severe temperatures gripping the state. That year though, the break in the weather was accentuated by severe electrical storms battering the northern towns of the state for two and a half hours, causing considerable damage.

Tragedy personally struck the Pilch's as well. Not to their livelihood but to the family of Chester's brother.

Francis Pilch's wife, Louise, had been enjoying the afternoon at Shaker Pines Lake with 11-year-old daughter Irene, 9-year-old son Paul, and a 10-year-old friend of the family, Warren Tarbox. As the storm began to hit the area the group hurriedly packed up and headed for home. Without warning a large tree limb broke from an overhead pine, landing on the passing vehicle. Rescuers had to use an acetylene torch to extract Louise and Irene from the wreckage. Both the young daughter and brother were swiftly removed to the nearby hospital in Springfield, Massachusetts, where Irene succumbed to her injuries.

Paul recovered fully but the family less so.

1946 ushered in the Chicken of Tomorrow contest, organized by the U.S. Department of Agriculture, with the backing of A&P (Atlantic & Pacific Company) and the support of every major poultry and egg organization in the country, all aimed at breeding a better big breasted chicken. The goal of the contest was, in the words of a 1947 Saturday Evening post article:

> *...one bird chunky enough for the whole family—a chicken with breast meat so thick you can carve it into steaks, with drumsticks that contain a minimum of bone buried in layers of juicy dark meat, all costing less instead of more.*

The contest itself was intense, with the first winners announced in 1948.

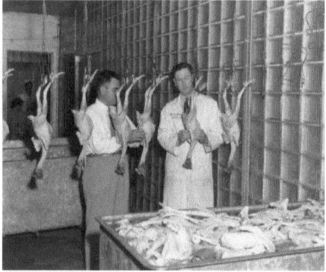

Judges evaluating 1948 Chicken of Tomorrow entries at the University of Delaware Agricultural Experiment Station. (courtesy the National Archives).

The first runner-up was Henry Saglio, the teenage son of Italian immigrant farmers in Glastonbury, Connecticut, who had bred his family's pure line of White Plymouth Rocks into a muscular, meaty bird which he raised on Abor Acres farm. Abor Acres was a direct competitor to Pilch's farm.

The winner was Charles Vantress from California, who had crafted a red-feathered hybrid out of a bird called *The New Hampshire*, the most popular meat bird among East Coast growers, and a California strain of Cornish. First prize carried a cash award of $5,000 ($53,000 in 2020).

The announcement was followed by a parade through Georgetown, Delaware, with floats depicting the phases of Delmarva's poultry industry and a smiling, waving Festival Broiler Queen perched on top of a car.

The only problem with the new "hybrids" was that the intricacy of the family trees breeders like Saglio constructed ensured that the birds could not be reproduced outside the companies that bred them. If a farmer who bought the new hybrids tried to mate them on his own property, the birds would not breed true.

To continue the line farmers were forced to purchase chicks form the source hatcheries.

Not to be outdone by his competition, Chester Pilch entered a White Cockerel in the 1953 regional Chicken of Tomorrow contest and walked away with First Prize for the heaviest entry in the history of the contest. The six- and one-half pound live bird easily outweighed the live competition by over one pound, and even outweighed them once it had been dressed.

> *A British couple who were in this country gathering poultry information in their travels, were so amazed at the terrific size of this outstanding bird, that they got up [at the event] and said that they had come over to see the eight and ninth wonders of the world and that the Pilch bird was one of them.[97]*

---

[97] Thompsonville Press. Sept 17, 1953. Pg 1.

FEEDING HILLS MAN BREEDING CONTEST BIRDS

Chester Pilch Enters 2 Settings In Chicken of Tomorrow Competition

By 1956 Pilch birds were being distributed all over the world, with two *European orders* sent to Italy and Ireland respectively. Breeding males were sent by ocean liner while the hatching eggs sent via airliner destined for incubators in each country. The Pilch White Rocks were famous for their rapid maturation as meat birds while the chickens' set records as egg layers.

In the September 26th edition of the Huntsville (Alabama) Times an article announced the purchase of a 500-acre state owned Talladega chicken farm by Pilch Chicks, Inc., of Hazardville, Connecticut for $70,000 ($781,000 in 2020).

REDS FOUL UP FLIGHT OF 70,000 BABY CHICKS FROM BRADLEY FIELD

Kansas Town May Move to Missouri as Result of Big Flood

Kansas City, Mo., April 28 (INS) —The Missouri River flood may have put Elwood, Kan., in Missouri.

Army engineers were to decide today whether to send off a new channel cut by the flooding river. If they don't, Elwood will be in the Show-Me State.

The town was inundated last week and all its 2366 residents were forced to flee their homes.

WAGE INCREASE OFFER MADE BY WESTINGHOUSE

Raises Would Range From One Cent Per Hour to $4.35 Per Month

Nearly 900 employees of the East Springfield works of the Westinghouse Electric Corp. are included in a wage increase offer made yesterday by the company from Pittsburgh.

For All Employees

The wages of 15,200 unionized salaried employees were raised, the Associated Press reported, and the same cost-of-living pay boost was offered to unions which represent 79,000 hourly-paid workers.

Salaried clerical workers get increases ranging from $1.76 to $4.35 a month, which would include about 500 here.

Pawns in New Red 'Incident'

Chester Pilch, left, of the Pilch hatchery, Hazardville, Conn., and Ralph Thresher of East Longmeadow, had no idea when they were checking a cargo of 70,000 chicks for Austria at Bradley Field yesterday that they were handling an international incident. Trouble developed when the Russians refused to extend permission for the Royal Dutch KLM transport to land after dark at Tulin field, outside of Vienna.

Russians Refuse To Let Airplane Land at Vienna

Birds Being Sent to Austrians Likely to Die Unless Fed Within 72 Hours; 13,000 Aboard Craft Are From Hazardville, Conn. Farm

A planeload of 70,000 baby chicks which began a 4000-mile flight to Austria from Bradley Field at 7.03 last night has become the latest source of irritation between East and West.

The International snag developed when the Russians refused to extend permission for the four-motored Dutch Royal Airline DC-4 to land at night. The plane, originally scheduled to land at Tulin Airport, outside Vienna, against a hangar.

Some 13,700 of the chicks, part of a total of 218,000 to be sent in three flights, are from the Pilch Poultry Hatchery in Hazardville, Conn.

After officials of Austria, the United States and the Dutch airline made a fruitless plea to the Russians to extend the permit, arrangements were made to land the plane at an American airfield near Linz, 117 miles west of Vienna.

The question remaining was whether the chicks could be hauled to

Continued On Page 7

Arvel Woodfin (A. W.) Todd, Alabama's Commissioner of Agriculture and Industries at the time, called the purchase the biggest shot in the arm for Alabama agriculture in years. The commissioner projected that Pilch would invest one million or more at the site over the two years following the purchase.

On January 26 of 1957 Chester Pilch was presented the deed to the Co-Operative Poultry Farm at Curry Station on the Anniston Talladega highway.

Todd exclaimed:

Alabama is the fastest growing state in the nation in the broiler business. In 1956 Our Alabama poultry industry grossed 91 million dollars, and was second only to cotton.

The broiler business is moving from the East to the South and Pilch couldn't locate a finer county in Alabama than in Talladega County.[98]

The expansion into the South would offer options to the company as a bargaining chip with Enfield in the future.

LOADING FOUR TONS OF CHICKS—Cargo handlers at Bradley Field yesterday are seen loading part of the four tons of chicks aboard a Dutch DC-4 which ran into a diplomatic storm when the Russians denied permission for the plane to land at night near Vienna. Supervising operations at right are, Walter Bishop, export company official, and Chester Pilch, extreme right, of Hazardville, Conn. The shipment is for the Austrian government.

By the end of the first month of 1957 the Thompsonville Press reported on the possibility of the Pilch's installing a light plane and helicopter pad at the Moody Farm location. The initial application had been submitted the previous Fall, and the site had been inspected the previous December. According to the State Department of Aeronautics the application would be approved in February, pending review by the Town of Enfield.

---

[98] The Anniston Star. January 6, 1957. Page 2.

The airfield was never constructed.

Meanwhile in Alabama Pilch was moving ahead renovating and upgrading the Talladega facilities and innovating in new ways to establish good will in the South. The Pilch hatchery, in concert with the Alabama Rehabilitation Service and the Alabama Institution for the Deaf and Blind, began a test of a new program to see if a modicum of self-reliance could be reestablished with the visually challenged.

In a first-of-its-kind initiative, Henry O'Neill, a married middle-aged black man who had lost his sight due to an industrial steel mill accident, was provided with a home for his family of eight and facilities for raising egg laying hens provided by the Pilch Talladega Hatchery. The goal for O'Neill was to successfully shepherd the poultry and return hatching eggs back to Pilch. If the project was successful, another group of 15 sight challenged people would be enrolled in the program.

The initiative was a success and expanded.

In August Chester Pilch was called to Washington, D.C to testify in front of the Food Industry Subcommittee of the Small Business Committee of the United State House of Representatives.

As one of seven invited poultry breeders he would offer his insights into the challenges of the industry.

Meanwhile, Francis was beginning to make his mark in the political arena, being elected to the Enfield Board of Education in November of 1957, replacing Carl Scavatto who had abruptly resigned his position. It would be an expansion of his *toe dip* into local government for Pilch, having previously served on the Hazardville Parent Teacher Organization, Hazardville Memorial School Addition Building Committee, and an active member of a committee looking to reorganize town government.

Within days of his election, he was also assigned to the High School Site Committee by the Board of Selectmen.

Five months later, in April of 1958, Francis Pilch became Secretary of the Democratic Town Committee as First Selectman Norbert Senio and Chairman Dominic Cimino combined forces to wrest control away from the opposition, assuring a more harmonious party line moving forward.

Pilch won his position in a majority 46-40 vote.

His political influence was expanding.

Down South, in August of 1958, as 19-year-old Pat Sanders was driving a busload of chicks he had just picked up from Henry O'Neill's mini-hatchery, a freight train broadsided the vehicle as Sanders crossed over the Southern Railway. Sanders was thrown from the bus, and chicks, both dead and alive, were scattered along the railroad tracks and roadway.[99]

Out at Moody Road Farm Chester Pilch worked hard at eliminating diseases which could wipe out his flock in a matter of days. These rules included showering and changing clothes when moving from one building to the next to maintain strict sanitary working conditions for the employees and environment for the chicks.

The Pilch Hatcheries were selling more than 10 million baby chicks annually. Despite the advantages of their Talladega operation Pilch decided to expand the offices of

---

[99] Anniston Star, August 5, 1958, Page 2.

the Enfield headquarters.

By April of 1962 Francis Pilch made his political move as he was elected Chairman of the Democratic Committee of Enfield by a vote of 44 to 41 over Charles Doyle. Pilch represented a *compromise candidate*, which simply meant he was acceptable to both factions of elected Democrats, neither of which held a majority.

As one of his first acts he announced a reduction of 1.5 in the mill rate for taxes, the first tax reduction in twenty years, an action which would predict future fiscal responsibility under his guidance.

That same year a four-alarm fire broke out at the Pilch Farm on Moody Road, which had begun in a washroom of one of the many one-story buildings. Tragically two thousand five hundred chicks were burned alive during the blaze, while the 350-foot-long administration building, which had only recently been expanded, was gutted.

Chester Pilch committed to reconstruction.

In October of 1963 the announcement broke that the Pilch Poultry Breeding Farms would be expanding northward by opening a hatchery in Saint Angele De Mannoir in Quebec, Canada.

Opening within the previous year were distribution centers in Smithfield, North Carolina, Texarkana, Arkansas, and Calistoga, California.

Continuing innovation, Pilch Broilers won an award for feed to meat conversion in the State of Maine Broiler Test begun in December of 1963. Chester Pilch predicted that within three years broilers could be commercially marketed two weeks earlier than they were at the time, which translated to farmers being able to produce six crops of birds per year instead of four - a fifty percent increase in sales poundage.

In an opinion article in the July 7, 1965 issue of the Thompsonville Press, Bill Brelsky commended the political chops of Francis Pilch as the town considered the idea of sewer expansion within the villages. Realizing that the program would be defeated, Pilch questioned the need for the expansion, while the Town Manager continued a hard sell of the program. In addition, Pilch labeled the referendum question as to appropriating monies for school construction before a site had been chosen as *ridiculous*.

Pilch reinforced his position as a voice for the common man.

Although his position was lauded by both the Springfield Daily News and the Hartford Courant, when asked for a response to charges made against his position by the Town Manager by the Thompsonville Press, Pilch responded:

> *If I told you anything you'd twist it so that the original meaning would be lost. Your paper is reporting this whole thing [sewer proposal] from one standpoint only, and not reflecting both sides of the problem or what people really think.*
>
> *Under the circumstances, I have nothing to say.[100]*

To revitalize Thompsonville after the departure of the W. T. Grant store at 35 Pearl Street in 1965, Chester Pilch proposed converting the vacant location into a chicken

---

[100] Thompsonville Press. Jan 6, 1965. Page 4.

hatchery. Pilch could not foresee any opposition based on the sanitary conditions of his other operations, and had, in fact, duplicated the same repurposing of sites in other towns in other parts of the country.

But shortsightedness in terms of maintaining a village's vitality spans generations, and so Town Planner William Kweder and Urban Renewal Master Plan consultant Sam Pine voiced their objections to the proposal.

Perplexed, Pilch voiced his exasperation:

Downtown Thompsonville is getting to be a ghost town. The planners are moving everything out, across the highway. Something has to change, and this can help.[101]

Pilch's roots were in Enfield, as well as his business, and he was looking for an opportunity to not only expand his operations but to employ up to 25 individuals at the proposed site. He had already been approached by several other communities to consider opening a hatchery elsewhere, one of which was Smithfield, North Carolina.

Chester did his best to convince the town planners of the many benefits of his proposal.

But they knew better.

The location remained empty, and the seeds of discontent had been sewn.

Pilch set up a hatchery in Smithfield, North Carolina.

In 1967 Pilch's Poultry Breeding Farm opened another hatchery below the Mason Dixon line in Iredell County, North Carolina.

For the first time the new plant was to be operated as a separate company called Pilch Amity Breeders, Inc. The

---

[101] Thompsonville Press. Sept 16, 1965. Page 3.

new site would employ 40 employees and would include two homes built for key personnel associated with the plant.

Much like the proposed reconfiguration of the W.T. Grant location in Thompsonville, which had been voted down, the new hatchery would be air conditioned and equipped with modern equipment. Separate areas would be constructed for egg setting, storage, incubation, hatching, and sorting.

Unlike Enfield, both R. D. (Shank) Warwick, Statesville Chamber of Commerce manager, and Harry Myers, Statesville Poultry Agent, stated that the new plant would help put Iredell County on the map as an important poultry breeding area, and that they were highly pleased that the company was locating their hatchery there.

In an aside to the rejected Enfield hatchery plans experience of 1965, Chester Pilch said that:

> ...it had taken the firm two years to determine a location for the plant and he didn't know of a finer location than that selected here. [We] like the place and the people and look forward to enjoying the hospitality of this area, as they plan to become an integral part of the community.

The warmth of the South versus the cool of the North.

Accommodation *and* weather.

Cuernavaca, Morelos, Mexico would soon be added as a hatchery location as well.

Three months later, in August of 1967, Pilch opened a hatchery outside of Dublin, Ireland, which would be tasked with supplying breeder chicks to both Ireland and England.

Pilch seemingly ruled the roost, which made his next play so out of character.

Japanese Distributors on Pilch Farms Visit

ENFIELD—Poultrymen from Japan who raise the Pilch breeder pullet yesterday viewed the Pilch Poultry Breeding Farms Research Center where the broiler meat bird originated. Chester Pilch, right, president of the international organization, is shown greeting the visiting poultrymen on their arrival at the Moody Rd. farm. The trip was sponsored by Tohzai Sangyo Boeki Co., Ltd., distributors for the Pilch organization in Japan.

In early August of 1969 both the Hartford Courant and the Thompsonville Press ran articles about the upcoming merger between Pilch's Broiler Breeding Farms of Hazardville, Connecticut, and Dekalb AgResearch of DeKalb, Illinois.

The new firm would become Pilch-DeKalb with Chester Pilch installed as Chairman of the Board and Carrol Christensen (of DeKalb) as General Manager. From a pure business standpoint, the marriage was made in Heaven.

Pilch had focused on chick production, projected to ship over a two billion in 1969, while DeKalb's specialized breeding program concentrated on developing hens which laid white eggs.

But the nagging question was "why merge"? Why sell when Pilch was at the top of their game internationally?

Perhaps that will be a question that will never have an answer.

Pilch-DeKalb To Move Operations To Iredell

Decision Revealed By Firm

R. D. (Shank) Warwick, general manager of the Statesville Chamber of Commerce, announced late Friday that Pilch-DeKalb, the world's second largest poultry-breeding firm, will move its home office from Pa...

Certainly, Pilch had hit continuous roadblocks in their attempts to expand their operations in Hazardville and Enfield. Initiatives had been stonewalled despite assurances from the Pilch's as to the benefits of their proposals to the community. In contrast the Southern States had bent over backwards to not only accommodate the poultrymen but to present themselves as willing and grateful partners, so Pilch had continued to expand their operations there.

Not surprisingly, Pilch-DeKalb announced in March of 1971 that they would be leaving Enfield later that year to relocate their operations to North Carolina.

High taxes and high labor costs were officially cited, but perhaps missed opportunities and bruised relationships were more of a factor.

People and businesses go where they are wanted.

The country's largest poultry breeder, and Pilch's stiffest competitor, Arbor Acres Poultry breeders of Glastonbury, Connecticut, remained in the state, despite the business issues cited by Pilch-DeKalb for their move.

Pilch-Dekalb weren't the only Enfield companies leaving for greener pastures in the South that year.

Bigelow-Sanford had declared their intent to close operations one month prior to Pilch-Dekalb's announcement.

A one-two punch to Enfield which stood to lose almost one thousand jobs, prompting the Town Manager of Enfield, Samuel Kissinger, to request the town be declared an *area of sudden rise unemployment* by the state's economic development agency. If the town was so designated it would be afforded, among other things, loans of 6% to businesses seeking to relocate into the area.

It just seemed sad that the town was hoping to be publicly identified as impoverished to stay viable when for years it had been home to two internationally recognized companies.

Now both were gone.

Maybe the anticipated urban renewal would help...

7: PUGILISTS

The February 7th, 1929, issue of the Thompsonville Press announced an upcoming night of amateur boxing planned by the Independent Amateur Boxing Club of Thompsonville for the 25th of the month.

Eight bouts of three rounds each were to take place in Wawel Hall, located on the second floor of the Polish National Home in Thompsonville.

The main event on that evening's card pitted "Babe" Oakes of New Britain against a local boy "Jimmie" Franciamore. Originally scheduled for three rounds, Franciamore knocked Oakes out in the second round to the delight of the partisan crowd.

The ring referee for the bout was nationally recognized former boxer "Philadelphia" Jack O'Neill (real name Charles Wysocki). The two judges scoring the event were Nicholas Nuccio and Thomas Whitely from the same neighborhood.

The evening was a success.

Eight months later new amateur boxing rules were

enacted the Connecticut State Legislature based on suggestions from the State Athletic Commission under the guidance of Thomas E. Donahue. The new guidance was an attempt to address both the tendency to promote professional matches under the guise of amateur exhibitions, and to protect true amateur athletes.

The rules included requirements that:

- boxers must wait seven days between bouts
- matches were limited to three rounds
- participants must be at least 16 years old, and
- all fighters had to be licensed by the state.

It was under this new guidance that the *second* match, billed as the *First* Amateur Night of Boxing at Wawel Hall, was held on September 16th, 1929. The Great Depression, which would grip the country for a decade, had already begun, but would not be officially recognized until the New York Stock Market crashed five weeks later.

The card, arranged by Stanley Jedzniak, state licensed promoter, and his assistant Frank Rypysc, included ten bouts of three rounds each. Wristwatches would be given to the winner of each amateur match.

Of particular interest to local fistic enthusiasts, was the scheduled middleweight match between "Kid" Turk and "Vinnie" Leone, regional boys, and bitter rivals.

The *Second* [Third] Amateur Night on October 11th is worthy of reprinting Thompsonville Press article.

Friday evening, October 11th, at the Polish National Hall, will be the scene of Thompsonville's second amateur fight program.

A night that promises the sporting blood plenty of thrills and action. Can amateur boxing survive in town will be answered that night. The management has done its share, the balance remains for the public to fulfill.

The best local talent has been booked to perform here. Boys who are known as real fighters.

First is the levelheaded and cool "Freddy" Albano, who has trained to meet the best man securable.

Next come boys from a fighting family. Carlo and John Angelica. Both boys are very fast and clever, Carlo being the local high school champ. Danny Reader, the pride of College Green, will make his initial bow as an amateur boxer. Joe Bonnelli, who has fought in the U. S. Army, will also make his bow to the public.

In Stanley Koziara the fans will see a boy who will go much farther than his hometown. Then comes the colorful "Frankie" Columbo of Windsor Locks. Columbo needs no introduction as he has fought here before. Jimmie martin will also be used against a worthwhile opponent. Last, but not least, is the colored flash from Suffield, a boy who has been eagerly sought by local fans, Boots Brewster, who will probably oppose either john or Carlo Angelica. The management wishes to inform the local boxing fans that only 546 seats are now available, and these are on sale through various agents of the Alore Boxing club.[102]

It proved to be a good night for the locals as Joe

---

[102] Thompsonville Press. October 3, 1929. Page 1.

Bonnelli, Danny Reader, Stan Kozara, Carlo Angelica, and Freddy Albano all won their matches.

Two weeks later, beginning on October 18th and culminating on October 29th, the bottom dropped out of the stock market, but neither the October 24th nor the October 31st edition of the Thompsonville Press reported on the event. In fact, in the November 7th edition of that same paper announced the purchase and assimilation of the Stephen Sanford & Sons, Incorporated Carpet Company by the Bigelow-Hartford Carpet Company, as if all was right in the financial world. In fact, the showing of carpet samples in New York on December 16th was crowded with buyers and ordering was brisk.

1929 ~ 1930

It wasn't until the middle of the following year that economic concerns made it to the front page of the newspaper. Depression had hit Thompsonville.

Depression had hit local boxing as well, as amateur fisticuffs had entered a period of "radio silence", with the lack of entertainment options broken only by a wrestling bout in the Fall of 1930.

On November 13, 1930, Fred Bruno (real name Frederick Anthony Poggie), the reigning light heavyweight wrestling champion of New England met the "Flying Frenchman" (William Peno) of Montreal, Canada, a the featured bout of three at Wawel Hall.

The expectation was, on the strength of the performance and expected attendance, that other matches would follow.

They did not.

1932

The thirst for local pugilism was finally quenched on

October 20, 1932, when two exhibition bouts were included as entertainment during the Boxing Club Dance held at Wawel Hall. The fistic club was under the direction of Ernest J. Bourque and membership included mostly Thompsonville residents who were boxing fans.

The event was a success, even in those trying times.

Perhaps boxing was due for a comeback.

And it did for one more event on December 2, in the high school auditorium, as part of another exhibition under the direction of Bourque. This time the proceeds of the event were turned over to the Visiting Nurses Association to benefit the organization's milk fund.

One of the boxers that evening who fought under the name Joe Dee, was a local boy, Joe DeMaria. Remember that boy's name.

1933

The July 13th, 1933, edition of the Thompsonville Press announced the long-awaited return of boxing to a hungry public in need of a distraction from the depression gripping the economy.

Under construction on Belmont Avenue for weeks on land owned by Gregory M. Sapsuzian, Jr., a new 3000-seat outdoor arena, [103] named for the Veterans of Foreign Wars (VFW), was ready to host ten amateur bouts of three rounds each.

Recognizing the challenging economic times, admission to the event was set at 25 cents for general admission and 40 cents for ringside.

---

[103] Note: Thompsonville Press correctly noted the new arena as a 3000-seat affair in its July 6, 1933, edition. One week later it misprinted the seating as 300 seats.

The matchmaker for the initial card was Ernie Bourque, whose Boxing Club had produced the boxing exhibition eight months earlier at Wawel Hall. This outdoor inauguration match included the reigning bantamweight champion of Connecticut and the Golden Gloves flyweight champion.

The opening show drew an estimated 1500 people from Thompsonville and the surrounding region, and did not disappoint in action, as the event included six knockouts.

Boxing was back, and attendee size would remain consistent for the rest of the summer and fall season until the final match on September 21.

The first fighter to step into the Belmont Avenue ring was a local boy Joe DeMaria [De Maria or Demaria or DiMaria] fighting under the name Joe Dee, who knocked out his opponent in the second round. He would go on to win most of his bouts over the next two years by knockout, until an injury in 1934 would force him to retire.

The country was still morally governed by Prohibition. Federal Agents and local police conducted a raid on an illegal still operation on land owned by Irving D. Woodworth and managed by Joseph Bartalotta, a local man who lived on Enfield Street. The illicit moonshining facilities, powered by a double steam boiler, included two large stills and five wooden vats, each with a capacity of 5,000 gallons of premium hooch.

The federal authorities believed that the operation was part of a multistate bootleg business with direct connections to mobs in Springfield, Massachusetts, upstate New York (the Catskill Mob), and New Jersey.

No connection was found between the VFW festivities personnel and the still operation, although one might question what had wet the whistle of the attendees or what might have fueled their unbridled enthusiasm besides their love of boxing.

1934

Thompsonville Arena boxing cards were still managed by Bourque while Gregory M. Sapsuzian, Jr., continued as event promoter.

The big buzz of the season was the possibility of a visit to the site by the former heavyweight champion of the world, Jack Dempsey. Politicians and fight aficionados were enamored by the prospect of the former champ attending a bout, but the increase in ticket prices needed to lure the pugilist to the Thompsonville Arena proved too costly, and negotiations were called off.

The mere possibility of a visit by the champion had raised the visibility of the arena to a regional boxing mecca.

1935

June 6th marked the opening of a new season at the VFW arena with Bourque and Sapsuzian still at the helm. One format change considered was the interspersing of professional bouts with amateur, although the first card included only amateur boxers.

In one bout a local pugilist fighting under the name of "Kid" Lamagna defeated Young Carpenter of Hartford.

Kid Lamagna, local battler, showed great improvement in winning decisively over Young Carpenter of Hartford. Lamagna threw too many gloves for the Hartford youngster in the first and third rounds.

Action started with the bell in this scrap, with Lamagna sending a number of hard rights to the chin of his opponent. His timing and coolness were major factors in his triumph.

It appeared for a moment in the third heat that the local woodchopper would finish the Capital City boy as he sent a series of punches to the chin and midsection, but Carpenter managed to hold on until the final gong.[104]

For the first time professional bouts were staged on July 3, 1935, at the VFW Arena on Belmont Avenue.

Concern among the promoters was whether the move to professional bouts would be received well by the loyal locals, so the first matches, which included three six-round and three three-round bouts, would help Sapsuzian decide.

Many of the fighters had previously appeared as amateurs, and their names were familiar to the partisan crowds. The featured bout matched light heavyweight Richie Thorer of Springfield, Massachusetts, who had fought as an amateur under the name "Kid" Richie, against an opponent from Westfield from the same state.

Thompsonville's professional entry, Johnny Vargus, would fight on the undercard.

Pro Fights To Feature At V. F. W. Arena Tonight

Three Six and Three Three Round Bouts Will Be Staged by Matchmaker Sapsuzian—Thorer to Battle Eddie Michaels in Main Go.

Weigh-ins took place at 2:00 at the Grey's Club, a popular sport associated hangout in Thompsonville.

---

[104] Thompsonville Press. June 13, 1935. Page 6.

One-week later Sapsuzian had his answer.

Only 900 cash customers attended the professional bout, down from the 1300 average.

Foremost Amateur Fighters Feature Card Here Tonight

Jackie Williams and Art McAlpine Collide in the Main Bout—Lou Blondie and Kid Lamagna, Local Boys, to Appear on Undercard.

Sapsuzian announced an end to the professional experiment, returning to the more successful amateur, hard hitting, action-oriented format.

It was as if the raw, untamed violence vented in the ring helped moderate the frustrations of the crowd as they continued to bob and weave against the economic punches of the Great Depression, and the amateurs were delivering the kind of action the fans required.

July 18th featured the amateur action the ring had become famous for, to the delight of the VFW audience.

> *A real topnotch bout will head the card featuring Jackie Williams, the Webster Bomber, and that sensational colored simon-pure fighter, Art McAlpine, who hails from the City of Homes [Springfield, Massachusetts].[105]*

---

[105] Thompsonville Press. July 18, 1935. Page 7.

Local boys Lou Blondie and "Kid" Lamagna were featured on the undercard.

In his weekly piece *Giving 'em the Once Over*, "Mac" Grey noted, in an interesting a piece that spoke more about racial biases than fisticuff talent:

Colored Boys Good Scrappers

One would get a little more enjoyment at the local amateur fights if he could stop in the locker room after the boys have performed their daily dozen. Especially if those two talented Negro fighters are present, namely Art McAlpine and Bobby Lawes. These boys are as amusing as one would desire to meet. It is interesting to listen to them crack jokes in their own dialect and they would undoubtedly make a couple of good end-men in any minstrel show.[106]

Over the following few weeks Lou Blondie kept up his winning ways, and a newcomer, "Al" Nabbo, began making a name for himself by running together a string of wins. Noticeably absent though, was local boy Lamagna.

In his column "Mac" Grey noted:

If Kid Lamagna isn't seen in action in the local ring very soon fight fans will be forgetting about him. It's about time that Lamagna was given a break on some of the coming boxing cards…There has been some talk about Lou Blondie being fed setups in order to enhance his record, but the truth of the matter is that the last two opponents who Blondie was slated to fight failed to make their appearance, which was the reason he took on the so-called "pushovers".[107]

---

[106] Ibid.

[107] Thompsonville Press. August 8, 1935. Page 7.

It's interesting on one hand that Grey proposes setting Lamagna up with some easy wins, while providing cover to Blondie against the same charge.

The August 15th, 1935, edition of the Thompsonville Press carried reports of Bigelow Carpet showing a loss for the past 6 months, William Clark still at large after escaping from Osborn Farm prison, and Golden Gloves Champions fighting atop of the VFW card in Thompsonville.

New York Golden Gloves Champs Top Card Tonight

Crack String of Gotham Performers to Feature Weekly Show—Williams, Blondie and Nabbo Also Show on Tonight's Program.

Perhaps more exciting though, was the announcement of Wrestling Matches to begin on Monday evenings at the Belmont Avenue Arena.

The first event, which was to be held on August 19th, would feature Tony Colesano of Springfield against Hans Schmidt of Germany. Colesano, the local Italian favorite, had made his name for himself over the previous year wrestling in regional tournaments.

Included on that evening's card were such notables as Red Dubuc, the Wild Frenchman; Max Piworski, the Polish Wizard; Jack Bloomfield, the Jewish Champ; and Lou Drenosky, the Hungarian Giant.

Boxing was not only back on Belmont Avenue, but attendance was growing, with a record high of 2535 fans in attendance set in the previous weeks.

Less delighted was wrestling promoter Sapsuzian, whose

grappling matches attracted only 250 fans, prompting the shelving of the venture.

The reviews were brutal:

> *It was the worst exhibition of wrestling that one could possibly witness, most of the performers failing to give even a good imitation of the game. It was plain to see they had not intentions of getting into the ring with the idea of giving the fans even a chance for their money's worth. Many fans that paid to get in were so disgusted with their exhibitions that they left before the card was completed.*

> *It was a wise thing that Promoter Sapsuzian has called a halt to them for it might have hurt his fine boxing shows that have begun to pack the arena.[108]*

Thankfully for Sapsuzian there was no carryover effect from the poor wrestling reviews on Thursday boxing as attendance for the following week was recorded as 2100 rabid fans. The attendees watched as local pugilists Blondie and Nabbo scored knock outs of their opponents on the same night, thrilling the audience.

September 12 marked the end of the 1935 boxing season, as Blondie, vying for the welterweight championship, fell to Ralph Zanelli, the reigning New England Champion.

It was the second meeting between the two, and Zanelli said it would be their last as he had no intention of going up against the local puncher again as the Rhode Islander said the Thompsonville native was the toughest opponent he

---

[108] Thompsonville Press. August 22, 1935. Page 7.

had ever faced.

Noted by "Mac" Grey in his column, a pugilist that hadn't been mentioned in months, Kid Lamagna, was reported to be rounding into form after a long layoff and would be ready to resume action in 1936.

All in all, it had been a wonderful year for the sport.

1936

The new season brought a new matchmaker to Belmont Avenue, Joseph DeMaria, a local Italian boy of 22 years. DeMaria had been the first boxer at the VFW Arena and had toiled under Bourque for years after hanging up his gloves, so he was a natural for picking up the matchmaking duties.

In new roles, Ernie Bourque and his brother Louie, of the Carpet City Boxing Club, were tasked with representing the amateur boxers of Northern Connecticut in the newly established *Managers' and Boxers' Protective Association.* The new group had been tasked with protecting a manager from having his stable of fighters lured away by a rival manager.

The sport was slowly maturing.

A new ruling attempting to quantify pugilists meant that Bourque's' group would be losing one of their best, as Lou Blondie had been ordered by the state commission to either retire or turn professional.

Another boxer, "Boots" Brewster of Suffield was given the same directive and would conclude his amateur career by meeting "Wop" Morelli on June 18, 1936. It would be the 81st amateur match for Brewster.

By July, it was clear that "Kid" Lamagna would never box again despite assurances from the previous year, and he officially retired from the game.

A favorite of the local crowd, Al Nabbo continued to refine his skills, but declared he wouldn't compete again until he had secured employment. It was a reminder that, as amateurs, these boys needed steady jobs to facilitate their pursuit of a career in boxing. It was also a reflection of the challenge of gaining employment in the middle of a national depression.

By the middle of July, the hammer came down from Connecticut's Boxing Commissioner Joseph Lawlor. The state had taken steps years earlier to crack down internally on professionals taking boxing matches as amateurs, but it was still a common practice in Massachusetts and Rhode Island where pros would fight under assumed names. Lawlor outright suspended three Worcester pugilists Al Costa, Tony Burke, and Edward Shapiro.

Attendance at the Belmont Avenue Arena held steady, with lows of 1200 and highs of 2500 attendees. The local economy seemed to be picking up steam as well, with 580 people removed from the town welfare rolls by the beginning of August, and the economic future seemed to be trending better.

Headed toward the end of the boxing season local boxer Al Nabbo, fighting now as the Thompsonville Flash, had yet to lose a fight, putting most of his opponents away with knockouts. In the final card of 1936 Nabbo would fight Julie Kogan, the Jewish Sensation from New Haven, who hadn't lost in the previous two years.

Who won the highly anticipated match?

There was no report in the following week's Thompsonville Press, leaving the reader hanging, as if he had been reading a mystery novel with the last page ripped from the binding.

1937

In April local boxing fans got an Easter gift as a new training facility opened on Main Street in Thompsonville. Promoter Sapsuzian and Matchmaker DeMaria were both in attendance at the unveiling and had prepared four exhibition bouts for the occasion. Former boxer Jerry Reale would be training both established and new blood, with two of the most promising Al Richards and Young Putriment hailing from nearby Hazardville.

The new fight club already had a membership of 70 hopefuls signed up and were continuing to accept applications.

A separate boxing gym at State Line, operated by Ernie and Louis Bourque, was a class affair with dimensions of 80 feet by 35 feet. Lou Blondie, who rumors had turning professional, was associated with the location, and there were rumors that the Bourque's would be constructing an arena in the area, but that was only speculation.

As Amateur bouts were about to begin on June 3, 1937, it was reported that the Belmont Street Arena had been expanded to afford over 3000 attendees a better view of the action as each successive row had been raised. 1936 had totaled over 40,000 attendees over the season, and Sapsuzian and DeMaria expected more in 1937.

> *During the course of four years, the Veterans of Foreign Wars Arena has become the leading fight center in Connecticut and Western Massachusetts. The caliber of the cards offered to the fans has been largely responsible for its growth. Action has been the keyword at the local arena, and that is just what the spectators have received.*[109]

---

[109] Thompsonville Press. May 27, 1937. Page 6.

Gregory M. Sapsuzian, Jr. (left) and Joseph DeMaria (right). Matchmaker DeMaria was often spelled Demaria, Dimaria, or DiMaria.

Locally the WPA began to expand the number of projects it was involved with, whether it was sidewalks in Hazardville, or sewer drainage in Thompsonville. In Hartford alone over 3600 people were involved in construction or reconstruction, all the while pumping needed dollars into communities and elevating the spirits of all employed in the efforts.

Deemed a financial and entertainment success once again, the 1937 boxing season ended with Al Ryll, a local favorite heavyweight boxer from nearby Southwick, Massachusetts, going toe to toe with Vic Galati of New Britain.

Galati had won his last three bouts, and had knocked "Tiny" Johnny Lesco, a massive fighter from Willimantic, out of the ring.

Following the match, Ryll would turn pro.

Al Ryll, heavyweight boxer from Southwick, Massachusetts.

But the close of the outdoor boxing season on Belmont Avenue didn't mean the end was at hand for boxing in 1937. Announced in the September 30th edition of the Thompsonville Press, boxing once again would move inside to Wawel Hall at the Polish National Home.

Attempted before without success, this time DeMaria believed he could make a go of it as there was no interruption between the closing of outdoor bouts and the launch of indoor.

Of note on the undercard Shadow Frangiamore of Thompsonville was to battle Adolph Hilter of Springfield, Massachusetts. The misspelling was a slight against the German dictator whose troops would roll into Poland twelve months later on September 1, 1938, essentially marking the beginning of World War II.

Although the attendance, 300, was not what DeMaria had hoped for, he went ahead with a second indoor card scheduled for the evening of October 7th with fingers crossed.

700 people attended the second attempt when 800 were needed to break even, so DeMaria made the difficult decision to halt the experiment.

Indoor boxing was down for the count, for the third time, as amateur fighting proved to be an outdoor sport.

1938

The new season, the seventh for the Arena, held a few surprises for Thompsonville fans. A new entry into the ring, local boy Vito Tallarita would make his boxing debut at 116 pounds against Young Berrie of Rockville. Tallarita would win by a decision and the event would mark the beginning of his long career associated with the sport.

Professional boxing was featured once again at the Belmont Arena opening, but this time only as a featured event alongside eight amateur matches. Previously professional bout attempts had replaced the entire amateur card and had failed to attract sufficient fans, and the experiment had been dropped.

This time though, combining both pro and amateur seemed to do the trick as the Arena was packed, and paved the way for bouts to come.

On July 7, 1938, Al Ryll returned to the VFW Arena as the leading heavyweight as crowned by Ring magazine. Ryll had made his debut as an amateur at Belmont Avenue, honing his skills in preparation for a professional career.

V.F.W. Arena's Largest Crowd Sees Ryll Score Decisive Win

2600 Rabid Fans See Southwick Heavyweight White Hope Punch Art McMahon Into Oblivion in Brief Fracas—Training Under Lou Brown Shows to Distinct Advantage.

Ryll did not disappoint, dropping Art McMahon to the canvas only 92 seconds into the bout. Several hundred fans were on hand from Gilbert and Barker of Springfield, Massachusetts, where Ryll had been employed while still an amateur before heading to New York to train under the well-respected Lou Brown. There Ryll had switched from southpaw to a right hander, initially bewildering his opponent and shocking the crowd.

It proved a worthwhile and beneficial change.

The following week nature matched Ryll's fury.

A storm of the greatest intensity ever known here and featured cyclonic winds which did tremendous damage throughout the community in uprooting trees, damaging buildings and a few automobiles, and ruining various substantial tobacco crops began last Friday afternoon at 3:30 o'clock. The storm lasted about 15 minutes, but did damage to tobacco alone estimated at $200,000. Other damage throughout the community was estimated at $40,000 [5.2MM *dollars in 2020].[110]*

A few weeks later Ryll was back at the Belmont Arena, reluctantly matched up against nationally recognized Paul Pross, who had recently defeated:

- George Brescia, the Argentine heavyweight champion
- Abe Simon, a 250-pound giant of a man, and
- Jim Robinson, 1937's Gold Glove winner and sparring partner of Joe Louis.

Despite the concern Ryll would win.

But even the attraction of local boy Ryll couldn't save the experiment of combining professional and amateur bouts. Professionals just didn't bring the sizzle that the crowds craved. The unpolished amateur boxers brought the kind of excitement that attracted fans, so once again, professional boxing was seemingly dropped at Belmont Avenue.

Meanwhile, the State Line Golden Gloves Boxing Gym [formerly the Sharkey Building] operated by the Bourque brothers as a training establishment in 1937, was garnering local and national attention as a fisticuffs facility.

The building, with an interior of 60' by 60', included a regulation size ring, arc lighting, and all equipment necessary to build and refine raw boxing skills.

One of Bourque's prized up-and-comers was Al Richer of Scitico, who was a hard hitter with either hand and the winner of 11 bouts in a row.

---

[110] Thompsonville Press. July 7, 1938. Page 1.

Then, just like that, professional boxing was back at the VFW Arena on August 18th. A bout between heavyweights Gene Ligarski and Shoemaker Grady, which had been controversially stopped by the referee two weeks prior was at the top of the card. In the previous meeting, just as Grady was about to go down for the count, the referee had awarded the bout to Grady which had incensed the crowd.

The continuing drama all but ensured a packed house.

The following week would see a return to an all-amateur card. But not just ANY card, as history would prove.

At the top of the fight card Charlie Baginski of Springfield would meet the national A. A. U. featherweight title holder, Ray Roberts of New York.

Born Walker Smith, Jr. in Ailey, Georgia, the boxer often fought under the name Roberts when competing as an amateur, even after capturing the national title. At 14 he attempted to enter his first boxing tournament but found out he needed an AAU membership card – so he borrowed one from another boxer who had recently quit the game whose birth name was Ray Robinson.

New York Boxers Head Fistic Card This Evening

Crack Colored Scrappers Appear in Top Bouts—Second Time in History of Local Arena That Such a Varied Array of Champions Will Appear on Same Card—Roberts and Baginski in Final.

Ray Roberts was Ray Robinson, the fighter who had the nickname 'Sugar" prepended to his boxing name by George Gainford, his manager and at whose boxing club he refined his skills.

So, on August 25th, 1938, Sugar Ray Robinson, the fighter that Ring magazine would cite as No. 1 in its ranking of the 100 Greatest Boxers of All Time, stepped into the ring at the Belmont Avenue Arena in Thompsonville, Connecticut.

Robinson lost.

N.Y. Amateur Champs at Arena Tonight

Crack Gotham Colored Scrappers who display their wares here this evening for the second time this season. They are as follows: Left to right: Bill Robinson, Ritchie Richards, Ray Roberts and Tanker Jones. Roberts collides with Charlie Baginski in main bout attraction.

"Colored" boxers from NYC. Sugar Ray Robinson is third from the left.

Two weeks later, Robinson and Baginski met in a rematch, the pugilist looking to avenge his loss.

Robinson fought Baginski to a draw. [111]

The following week a hurricane swept through Thompsonville, exceeding the damage of the year's earlier storm, and the local paper was published in an abbreviated form. Even with that it was able to report the terrible toll it

---

[111] Thompsonville Press. June 29, 1939. Page 7.

had taken on the town – the worst in the 258 years of the town's history.

The 1938 boxing season was over.

Hurricane Sweeps Town Property Loss Terrific

Damage Estimated at Hundreds of Thousands of Dollars---Streets Throughout Town Piled High With Wreckage and Uprooted Trees---Phone and Power Service Crippled---No Lives Lost, No' Serious Injuries Reported---Flood Recedes.

1939

Sugar Ray Robinson, fighting as Ray Roberts, couldn't get enough of Thompsonville.

At the opening of the Belmont Arena the A.A.U champion fought Charlie Baginski once again, this time winning decisively.

The next time Robinson fought he was pitted against Eddie Mientka of Springfield, with the New Yorker winning once again.

> *The New York colored boy is undefeated in his last 37 bouts, to hold one of the longest win streaks an amateur lightweight has ever held. Eddie Mientka defeated Cher O'Rourke of Worcester in the main bout here two weeks ago, and showed plenty of improvement as a boxer from last year. Roberts means business and will be out to kayo the Springfield lad.*[112]

On July 13 Robinson went up against George (Red)

---

[112] The Thompsonville Press. June 29, 1939. Page 7.

Doty of Hartford. Regional papers reported it as the outstanding amateur bout in the country, and expectations were high as Doty had knocked out Baginski in his previous match and wanted Robinson or no one.

Doty, who had his amateur status extended by the Connecticut Boxing Commissioner until the following September, promised a knockout of the New Yorker.

Doty lost.[113] On the undercard Vito Tallarita won again.

On August 10 Robinson was at it again at the 3000 seat Belmont Avenue Outdoor Arena.

> *Ray Roberts of New York City, amateur lightweight champion of the world, will be in the feature bought on the amateur card at the V.F.W. Arena this evening. Roberts draws as his opponent, Chet O'Rourke of Worcester. O'Rourke is one of the hardest hitters among all of New England amateurs, with several kayo victories to his credit, and Ray Roberts also is a good hitter, and a master ring man, hence tonight's meeting at the Belmont oval looms as one of the most promising of the current season.[114]*

Robinson won. On the undercard, Tallarita of Thompsonville won as well.

The season would end in early September as regionally popular fighters rounded out the remaining cards, such as "Tanker" Jones, national heavyweight champion from NYC, Ed Baldwin, heavyweight champion of CT, Al Richards of Hazardville, "Wild Bull" Budynkiewicz, "Spider" Williams, "Kid" Chil, "Roughhouse" Vivienzo,

---

[113] Hartford Courant. August 7, 1974. Page 2C.
[114] The Thompsonville Press. August 10, 1939. Page 7.

"Kid" Shumac, and Johnny Riley of Thompsonville.

Riley was awarded the main bout on the final card based on his rating as the best amateur boxer in Connecticut. He would be matched up against "Red" Doty of Hartford, who had delivered the only knockout of Charlie Baginski's career, something that even Robinson had failed to do.

1940

The new season opened with the noticeable absence of Ray Robinson [Roberts] as the former amateur had turned professional.[115] One fighter though, beginning to make a name for himself locally was Vito Tallarita.

> *In another bout Vito Tallarita, a 118 pounder, will clash with Gus Levine of New York. Levine is known as the Jewish boy from New York. Tallarita has shown an improvement of one hundred percent over last year, and in his starter last week, beat "Roughhouse" Vivienzio.*

In a real slight to the now professional Robinson, write 'Mac" Gray, of the Thompsonville Press, was at it again.

> *Ray Roberts, the crack amateur boxer from New York who performed at the local fight arena the last two summers, was seen in action on the screen at the Strand [local movie theater in Thompsonville] last week. Roberts was seen boxing his way to the title in the New York Golden Gloves Tourney. It was more impressive watching him on the screen than in the local*

---

[115] Norwich Bulletin. January 3, 2009. Bill Stanley *Pep In Norwich*. (reporter interview with former champion Willie Pep). *Sugar Ray fought under the name of Ray Roberts. Ray always used that name when he fought in the amateurs.*

ring.[116]

Strangely sports reporting seems to take an extreme hit in the 1940 Thompsonville Press. After an opening season

To Honor "Milt" Piepul At V. F. W. Arena This Evening

MILTON "TARZAN" PIEPUL

By "MAC" GRAY

article, future reports are relegated to minor mentions in the **Personals—Social events—Club and Society Items** section of the paper. That is until the August 15th issue when the VFW is feature on the front page, but only because a local sports star Milton "Tarzan" Piepul was being honored that evening at the Belmont Avenue Arena.

This evening fans from Thompsonville and surrounding cities and towns are going to give Piepul the warmest reception he has received since he was honored with the football captaincy of Notre dame, a traditional honor in perhaps the greatest university in the country when football is mentioned.

Matchmaker Joe DeMaria proved today he wasn't kidding when he said he would make the Milt Piepul testimonial amateur fight show tonight in the Veterans of Foreign Wars Arena by signing Benny

---

[116] The Thompsonville Press. April 4, 1940. Page 2.

Hagen pf Springfield, and Emery Demers of Ware, in a rematch as the semi-final to the Mike Delaney – Joe Gans feature. DeMaria is going all the way to make the testimonial show the best of the year.[117]

The following week the boxing report was once again an afterthought buried in the **Personals—Social events— Club and Society Items** section of the paper.

Perhaps the events unfolding in Eastern Europe were taking more of the nations and newspapers attention as Germany invaded, Denmark, Norway, Belgium, the Netherlands, and Luxembourg, while Italy invaded southern France, and the Soviet Union captured Romania, Estonia, Latvia, and Lithuania.

The United States formerly entered the war one year later in December of 1941.

1941

The 1941 season opened with DeMaria taking on the role of Promotor/Matchmaker. The reason for Sapsuzian's absence is unclear. DeMaria announced a competition for a renaming of the Foreign Wars Arena, soliciting suggestions from fans during the season. It is unclear as to whether there was ever a winner of the competition.

In July respected promoter Homer Rainault leased the Thompsonville Arena for a series of professional bouts, interspersed with amateur affairs. Joe DeMaria would continue as matchmaker for Rainault.

The first professional bout produced under this collaboration matched Puerto Rico's greatest ring product, Eddie "Primo" Flores, with Carmelo Fenoy of Barcelona,

---

[117] The Thompsonville Press. August 15, 1940. Page 5.

Spain.

In August the town was abuzz when it was announced that Hartford product Willie Pep would meet Flores in the Belmont Avenue ring. Pep was unbeaten at the time, with 35 straight wins under his belt.

Scheduled to go eight rounds, Pep made quick work of Flores, knocking the 124-pounder out with a right cross to the head followed by a left hook.

The Puerto Rican native dropped to the canvas for a full count at two minutes and thirty seconds of the first round.

The Thursday night cards continued to feature both Pro and Amateur bouts, intermixed on the evening cards throughout the season.

1942 ~ 1945

The war years took their toll on the Belmont Avenue Arena as it was void of any action as key individuals DeMaria, Tallarita, Lamagna, and others entered various arms of military service in support of the United States and the efforts against Germany, Italy, and Japan.

1946 ~ 1947

Finally, a glimmer of fisticuffs hope as Vito Tallarita and Ray Fisher received their honorable discharges from their respective military service. In a March 7, 1946 article, the venerable reporter "Mac" Gray announced that boxing will return to the outdoor arena at the VFW. Fisher would serve as promoter, replacing Sapsuzian, and Tallarita as matchmaker, replacing DeMaria.

The format for the new season would be semi-professional, which simply meant that the boxers would be compensated, not so much so they could survive without other income, or not at all as in amateur bouts.

On June 6th, 1946, after a long dry spell, boxing returned to Thompsonville, and once again took its place on the front page.

> *With advance reservations pointing to a capacity crowd, outdoor boxing returns to the VFW Arena here tonight when promoter Ray Fisher and matchmaker Vito Tallarita present a semipro card which they believe will produce enough action for the most exacting fans.*

> *Fighters who saw plenty of action in service bouts are featured and a trio of five-round bouts are arousing much interest among patrons of the popular outdoor club.*[118]

Capacity or near capacity crowds formed week after week for the entire season, quenching the thirst for local fight fans.

Sports reporting though, was not as robust as in the previous decade. Some weeks the Thompsonville Press

---

[118] The Thompsonville Press. June 6, 1946. Page 1.

went front page with specifics of the upcoming bouts, while other weeks the card was not even mentioned. Perhaps it was a refocus on revenue generation and reprinting less costly subscription news reports rather than sharing local sports information that was deemed less important than content fillers (*see below*).

1948 ~ 1949

Stand Back, Ladies!

CHEYENNE, WYO. — A bill requiring women to stand five feet away from bars when drinking in public was introduced at the present session of the state legislature.

Retired Railroad Man To Run Model Train

PHILADELPHIA.—After 45 years as a railroad man, Allen R. Wilson has decided to retire so he can devote more time to his hobby. From now on he will operate his miniature railroad, including 400 feet of track, several locomotives and plenty of cars. He even has a railroad bridge, a reminder of the years he spent designing them for the Pennsylvania railroad.

In January of 1948, Angelo Lamagna, who for years had fought under the ring name "Kid" Lamagna, was completing preparations for the first youth boxing tournament to be held at the Enfield High School auditorium. Lamagna and Joseph Krzys had been instructing the young club members on the finer points of fisticuffs and had divided the boys into two groups – one representing the Northend and the other the Southend of town.

Vito Tallarita would referee the 12 matches. One of the ring judges was Thompsonville Press's own "Mac" Gray.

The 1948 and 1949 seasons continued to offer the hungry patrons a weekly dose of fine boxing, albeit drawing from Hartford, Springfield, Groton (submarine base), and New York City. There was less of a distinctive local feel to the matches, but both years were successful, nonetheless.

1950

On August 3, 1950, wrestling was reintroduced to the arena under the guidance of the John Maciolek of the American Legion Post 154. The matches would continue until the close of the season, offering up such names as "Roughouse" Fred Carone, the "Canadian Lumberjack", "Two Ton Tony Galento", "Comical Bad man from the South of the Border", "Tiger Tasker", and the "Golden Bear".

1951

1951 marked a change as Vito Tallarita shifted his matchmaking allegiance to the Mount Carmel Boxing Arena on Park Avenue in Thompsonville. Promotion for the events were handled by the Mount Carmel Society, with free onsite parking offered to all patrons.

The Thompsonville Arena on Belmont Avenue was still a viable option, and Joe DeMaria was handling the matchmaking for the outdoor cards there coupled with Promoter Sapsuzian. 1951 was billed as the 19th campaign for the site, and the arena had undergone a complete renovation.

Wrestling was offered up at the Belmont location as well, with the popular sport capturing the Saturday evening slot at the Thompsonville Arena. The sport began to capture a dedicated audience, attracting competitors from Canada, Boston, New York, and Ohio...and from overseas, the Portuguese champion as well.

The third week offered up "midget wrestling" as if the sport needed to become any more unique.

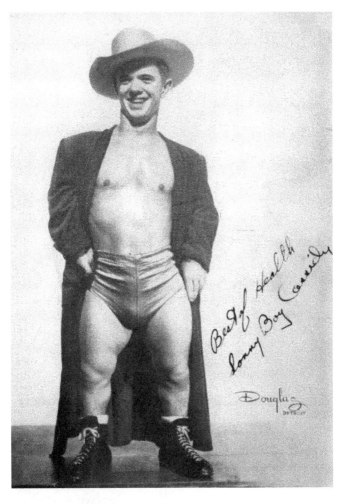

Sonny Boy Cassidy. America wrestler standing at four feet one inch.

The Mount Carmel bouts ran opposite the Thompsonville matches, both events presented on Thursday evenings. It made for an uncomfortable arrangement between the former collaborators. The local paper presented robust articles on the front page of the paper for each site, as if it was taking delight in the arena competition.

Each site attempted to "out point" the other, which made for a more enjoyable experience for the crowds. On July 5th, 1951, the Thompsonville Arena actually held a 12 round regional professional bantamweight bout to determine the New England champion, as the crown was vacant. At the opposing Mount Carmel Arena, the paper reported the presentation of a "Snappy Card" opposite the Belmont Avenue offering.

The following week Tallarita put on three New York Gold Glovers at Mount Carmel while DeMaria elected to go with an all-amateur ticket featuring local talent.

So it was – back and forth.

July 19 saw DeMaria match "Bom-Bom Oriental", the Cuban lightweight champion against Teddy "Redtop" Davis of Hartford who was managed by Willie Pep, in a scheduled eight round feature bout. Mount Carmel switched their matches to Tuesday nights, with Wednesdays as rain backups.

Saturdays at the Arena were the province of wrestling.

THOMPSONVILLE ARENA
BELMONT AVENUE—THOMPSONVILLE

TONIGHT--BOXING
ALL STAR BOXING SHOW

SATURDAY–WRESTLING
TAG TEAM AND TWO OTHER BOUTS

New to the format was the introduction of tag team

wrestling, which had begun to take the country by storm.

In addition to the free press boxing was afforded by the Thompsonville Press reporters, the Arena began to take out paid advertising to increase their visibility.

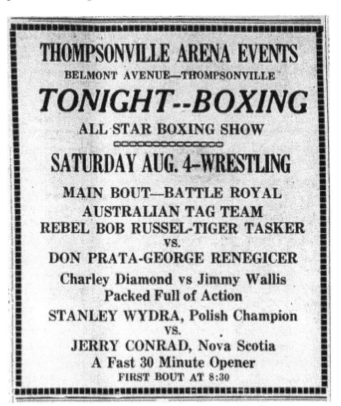

The move to Tuesday fights seemingly hampered the Mount Carmel Arena attendance as the print dates and frequency of the local weekly didn't afford free promotion by sports reporting of the events held early in the week.

Neither the July 4th nor any August newspapers made mention of the Mount Carmel Arena Tuesday matches as if the Arena had disappeared. The Thompsonville Arena continued to advertise.

The Hartford Courant did mention the results of the August 28th matches at the Mount Carmel Arena, noting the attendance was a dismal 800.

With that the 1951 season came to a close, both arenas claiming victory. There would be no boxing at the Mount Carmel site the following year, which affirmed Thompsonville's claim as the venue of choice.

1952

1952 marked the 20th season for the Belmont Arena festivities, and Joe DeMaria, now co-promoting alongside Greg Sapsuzian, continued the Thursday night fights and Saturday night wrestling matches.

The first fight of the 1932 inaugural season had featured DeMaria, boxing as Joey Dee, as the very first bout at Belmont Avenue. He won that fight with a knockout in the second round. DeMaria gave up his career inside the ring in favor of becoming one of the best matchmakers the area had ever seen, and 1952 would prove to be one of his better years.

He had shut down the competing ring, at least for the short term, and the boxing fans had been treated to some stellar events because of the rivalry the year earlier. The only week not filled with boxing would be Memorial Day weekend in honor of the veterans and the festivities surrounding the holiday.

Once again tag team wrestling seemed to be what the wrestling fans longed for, and DeMaria was more than willing to promote winning cards. On the boxing end, the local Westover Air base provided pugilists that proved both worthy and entertaining.

BOXING TONIGHT

THOMPSONVILLE ARENA

BELMONT AVENUE — THOMPSONVILLE

SLAM BANG AMATEUR BOUTS

WITH PLENTY OF TOP RING ACTION

— FEATURING —

4 Canadian Champs

PLENTY OF SLAM BANG ACTION

FIRST BOUT AT 8:30

1953

A big change came to the Thompsonville Arena in 1953 as a new promoter and matchmaker signed a lease to manage boxing shows at Belmont Avenue.

Sam Gallino [Gulino], a Hartford gym proprietor announced his outdoor boxing schedule which began on June 16th and would continue each Tuesday evening for the rest of the season. The format would mirror those of previous years.

Something beyond a change in promoters was at hand as the crowd size varied between 300 and 800 fans for a 3000-seat arena. Maybe it was due to an "outsider" handling promotion and matchmaking while drawing regional boxers to fill the card rather than local boys. Gulino was having trouble as well in having boxers withdraw or be no-shows at the ring – a bad look for a matchmaker.

The noticeable drop-off in coverage from the Thompsonville Press didn't help things, with articles posted inconsistently, and virtually no advertisements inside the paper. The Hartford Courant stepped in and picked up the slack, reporting on upcoming bouts as well as providing match results.

By August the Press returned to reporting on the local bouts at the Arena, the renewed interest in the sport made more baffling for its previous absence. Perhaps it was the appearance of Thompsonville lightweight Buddy Provencher, a National Guard member, who had rung up a string of six knockouts of his previous eight bouts.

In late August, DeMaria, a familiar name in the sport, partnered with Gulino in promoting and matching the Arena fights. But it wasn't the same historical matchmaker Joe DeMaria but his brother Pete, who hoped to bring back some fisticuffs magic and excitement to the area.

In one of Pete DiMaria's[119] first moves, Billy Lynch of Hartford was convinced to turn professional, as it had proved near impossible to sign any amateurs from the tri-state region to take him on. Lynch, a 135 pounder, won his first fight, a four-round decision over a more experienced fighter. Including his amateur bouts, Lynch hadn't lost in over a year.

In his second professional bout, Lynch won again, on a knockout. It seemed as if Gulino had a tiger in his stable.

After the Thompsonville Arena closed for the season Gulino brought his boy to New Britain, where the fighter won again, in a November bout against Rocky Sullivan.

1954

On June 10th the Thompsonville Arena stood alone as

---

[119] Yes – the brothers spelled their last name differently

the sole boxing venue in the town with Pete DiMaria acting as Promoter and Vito Tallarita returning as Matchmaker.

The duo was dynamic, signing up bouts that other regional arenas had only hoped for, and drawing the kind of crowds that reminded folks of the 1930s. Not only was boxing back but so was wrestling, whether mano-mano, tag team, or midget.

Appearing multiple times at Belmont Street was

Gorgeous George [George Raymond Wagner] of Hollywood, California, who was one of the biggest wrestling stars of the sport. He had garnered massive media attention for his outrageous character, which was described as flamboyant and charismatic, and the Thompsonville crowds ate it up.

On the wrestling card later in the year Leo Arnone, at the time a policeman on the Enfield squad, made his wrestling debut against Buddy Gilbert of Brooklyn, New York. Although new to the professional wrestling sport, Arnone had wrestled while in the Marines defeating some of the best matmen on the island of Guam.

Stirring up excitement in town, Arnone won his debut match and was awarded the opportunity to wrestle...

> ...a former German Storm trooper of World War II, Fritz Von Wallick of Munich, Germany in a 20-minute special match. Promoter Pete DiMaria and matchmaker Tallarita both feel that Arnone can make the grade as an outstanding wrestler and are doing everything possible to keep Leo active so he can develop into a star.[120]

Arnone defeated the German. After the bout a New York City promoter approached Arnone and offered the policeman matches in the New York area.

---

[120] The Thompsonville Press. August 19, 1954. Page 1.

In what proved to be the last card of the 1954 season, two featherweight boxers who had fought to a draw three times previously, Art Lupo of Hartford and Rocky Dion of Holyoke, Massachusetts were awarded the title bout with the winner getting a special award, most likely for determination and stamina.

1955

On May 26, a front-page article in the Thompsonville Press announced the sale of the 3500 seat Thompsonville Arena on Belmont Avenue by its owner, Greg Sapsuzian to the residential land developers Clarence and Raymond Provencher.[121]

Sapsuzian, the former promoter, blamed low turnout for the sale, but that really wasn't supported by the previous year's attendance numbers. The culprit was more likely rising land values and possibly a reluctance by the landowner to continue the venue.

There was more than the mere dismantling of a boxing arena that took place on Belmont Avenue.

As the stands and ring were demolished and clouds of dust and debris filled the air one could almost hear the roar of the crowd as Diciantes hit Pasquale so hard that the latter gave up boxing, Roberts peppering Doty with lefts and rights, knocking the Springfield native to the canvas three times until the fight was stopped, and Tallarita and Lamagna responding to the cheers of the Thompsonville loyalists.

When the last of the arena was carted away there was nothing left but memories, soon to be replaced by ranch-style homes and young families, oblivious to the history that lay beneath their feet.

---

[121] The Thompsonville Press. May 26, 1955. Page 1.

8: SON OF A GOOD FELLA

It began with a toxic competition between Thomas A. Edison and George Westinghouse over which type of generated electricity was safer and more efficient.

Edison was convinced that Direct Current would best serve the power requirements of the country, whereas Westinghouse, who had licensed Nicholas Tesla's technology, was sure Alternating Current was superior.

The rivalry was intense and bitter with the electrification of the nation at stake.

For Edison, hope appeared in the form of Alfred P. Southwick, a dentist from Buffalo, N.Y., who believed electricity could provide a more humane way to execute condemned criminals.

At first Edison rejected Southwick's overtures, directing him instead to Westinghouse who did not want his generator's associated with execution, as it would set a bad precedent and would associate Alternating Current with Death.

Coming to a similar conclusion as to the power of negative press, Edison contacted Southwick and informed him he would underwrite the construction of New York's first electric chair, employing not his own but rather Westinghouse's Alternating Current technology.

An undeniable method to Edison's madness.

While Edison paid for the chair, Westinghouse paid for the defense of the condemned criminal William Kemmler, in hopes of staving off his execution and the use of Southwick's electric chair.

But Westinghouse lost, as did Kemmler. Which would suffer the most was still to be revealed.

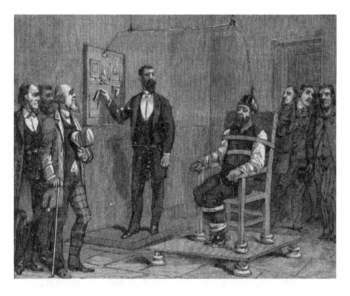

August 6, 1890 artist rendering of first execution by electric chair (artist unknown)

On the fateful day Kemmler was strapped down to a wooden chair, electrodes affixed to his head. A switch was thrown and electricity from an alternating current generator coursed through Kemmler for 17 seconds.

As the power was cut two attending physicians

pronounced the convict dead.

And then Kemmler inhaled.

The "dead man" was alive, his heart still beating.

Horrified, the prison administrators turned on the power for the second time; Kemmler stiffened in response.

For four long minutes Kemmler twitched and cooked.

When the power was disconnected there was no doubt that the prisoner was dead.

Some witnesses fainted as they watched.

Others had run from the room vomiting from the stench of burning flesh.

Newspaper reports were not kind.

Westinghouse was horrified.

Edison was gleeful.

The cards were always easier and kinder to Salvatore Bonelli than life was. Born in Naro, Italy, on May 8th, 1883, he emigrated at the age of 23 from the port of Palermo, arriving at Ellis Island aboard the Sicilian Prince in 1906.

Bonelli settled in at 17A River Street in Thompsonville with his wife Calogera and his two children, son Joseph and daughter Calogera. He took a job as a dyer in the carpet mill. Living with the young immigrant family were his Mother-In-Law Angelou Bento and Sister-In-Law Josephine Bennice.

Even with four adults in the home tragedy was not averted as, only one year after their arrival, Bonelli's two young children, playing unattended in the kitchen, pulled a large pot of boiling water from atop the stove onto themselves. The youths' screams alerted their parents, who called local doctors to attend to the suffering children.

The youngest daughter died the next morning from her burns. Joseph survived.

The family misfortune did little to mollify Bonelli's character, as he had, in a very short time, established himself as a thug with the local authorities. In contrast though, Salvatore had endeared himself to his Italian neighbors, the Raccios, Costas, Gioardinas, Passalacquas, Delgaizos, and Volpes as a man who *had their backs*. They had his as well, as they demonstrated after Bonnelli had smacked Vinnie (Vinchenzo) Porchello around a little for cheating him at cards, and, in an act of quick revenge, Porchello's son John shot Bonelli in the forearm in a Thompsonville alley.

> *Porchello then fled to his home on Windsor Street, followed by an excited, shouting mob, who surrounded the house and were rapidly gaining in numbers and excitement when the police arrived.[122]*

Abbiamo tuo fratello le spalle.[123]

By 1918 Bonelli had moved to 65 West Street in Thompsonville and had taken a job as a laborer at the Springfield Armory in Massachusetts, as reflected in his WWI registration card.

The small-time hood's influence and *business* relationships had extended from his Thompsonville neighborhood to his workplace and beyond. In 1921 Bonelli was sought by police in connection with an explosion and fire which had destroyed a house in Palmer, Massachusetts,

---

[122] Thompsonville Press. March 7, 1912. Page 4.
[123] We have your back, brother.

some 30 miles from his Connecticut residence.

The primary suspects in the arson case were Ginaldo Ignazio, a neighbor of Bonelli's in Thompsonville, and Cologero Simraglio and Cologero D'Geranni, who had occupied the dwelling at the time. Bonelli, unlike the others, was never charged in the case, but the police knew *where there's smoke, there's fire.*

Two years later Salvatore was using an *Americanized* version of his name, and, as Sam Bonelli, owned and ran a store of suspect nature at 28 Pleasant Street.

Prohibition had been instituted in 1920, but the law hadn't done much to tamp down local thirst for spirits and based on a raid at Bonelli's store on October 25, 1923, Sam was doing his best to fill that void. His establishment would remain a place of interest for the Thompsonville police and would be raided frequently for years.

Bonelli continued as a minor irritant to the local Boys in Blue for the next decade.

On November 16, 1935, Bonelli set a new arrest record even for himself by getting cuffed on two separate occasions within 24 hours because of a dispute at the Independent Social Club in Thompsonville.

Bonelli had accused Sam Mancuso, a gambling friend, of cheating during a card game. He'd done this with other players before, but this time Bonelli stabbed the gambler twice in the side with a pocketknife for good measure. Bonelli was taken into custody, charged, and released.[124]

The following morning the minor league gangster was recaptured and charged with assault on Joey Arnone, as the knifing of Mancuso perhaps hadn't been enough to send a

---

[124] Thompsonville Press November 21, 1935. Page 2.

greater message to those who weren't honorable card players.

When Bonelli appeared in court for the crime he paid a fine of 25 dollars with court fees of 23 dollars and 21 cents. A 60-day jail sentence was also imposed, but later suspended.

Judge Guy F. Bushnell, brother of the First Selectman Ira, lived on Enfield Street in Thompsonville and presided at the local court. He seemed to be what one might have called a sympathetic judge.

In the same year Salvatore Bonelli emigrated to the United States, 28-year-old Carlo De Caro of Naples, Italy, crossed the Atlantic on board the S.S. Weimar, arriving at Ellis Island, New York on March 17, 1906, with a final destination of Thompsonville, Connecticut.

Four years later he married Paulina (Apolonia) Kot of Galacia, Poland, who had emigrated in 1907, also settling in Thompsonville having been sponsored by Wiktorya (Victoria) Gasior, a local girl of Polish descent.

De Caro's oldest brother Ludovico (Louie) had preceded Carlo to the United States by three years with older brother Nicholas preceding Louie by two years. Younger brother John had followed his siblings soon after.

All had settled in Thompsonville.

Carlo and Paulina had five children; Lucia in 1910, Andrew in1912, Cesare in 1917, Carlo Jr. in 1924, and Raymond in 1926.

The couple purchased their first house on Park Avenue in Thompsonville, which included a bare lot, from Cologero Arnone, Mary Carcasola, and Rose and Grace Arcadipane in 1923, moving the family of four into the two-family home.

The De Caro families, for the most part, seemed to be staying out of trouble with the law, except for minor traffic accidents which plagued each of the brothers, none of which resulted in fatalities or jail time.

Prohibition though, seemed to bring out the entrepreneur in each of them, and in 1923 the stores of Louis De Caro and brother Nicholas were unsuccessfully raided.[125]

For two years the De Caro's continued to capture the attention of the police as well as the fire department and insurance companies. At one point Louie's *fruit and confectionary store* on Pleasant Street, long suspected of selling liquor, experienced a fire of suspect origin. Above the establishment the Independent Social Club regularly met, and gambling was suspected there, but no arrests were made as perhaps it kept the activity localized.

Two weeks after the fire the police returned to the same store, arresting Carlo De Caro Sr., who was minding the store for his brother Louie, for selling liquor from the establishment. De Caro was fined and released.

In an article titled **The Bootlegging Industry Also Shows Brisk Revival** in the January 21st, 1926, issue of the Thompsonville Press, the writer bemoaned the rise of illegal liquor sales in the town, going so far as to drawing a line between "good" and "bad" bootleggers.

That same year Frank Pilch, another resident of Pleasant Street, who years later would serve as Chairman of the Enfield Democratic Party, was pinched at his home with two gallons of moonshine and charged with intent to sell. Pilch's wife had been charged with the same offense in 1925 thus making the enterprise a family affair.[126]

---

[125] Thompsonville Press January 22, 1925. Page 1.
[126] Thompsonville press January 21, 1926. Page 8.

Pleasant Street was garnering a lot of police attention, as Nicholas De Caro's store was raided once again on Saturday, February 19th, the proprietor arrested and charged with keeping liquor with the intent to sell. This time De Caro was sentenced to 90 days in the Hartford County Jail as it was the bootleggers second offense.

DeCaro Declares That He Will Return As A State Or Federal Officer and Clean Up Town

FOLLOWING his conviction for "bootlegging" in the Enfield Town Court last Saturday morning, Nicholas DeCaro of Pleasant Street startled the court officials and attendants who were within his hearing with the following declaration: "I'll take my medicine and serve my time, but when I get out I will return here as a state cop or a federal agent and clean up the town." DeCaro had been just sentenced to serve 90 days in the Hartford County Jail and paid a fine of $400 with costs. "Nick," as he is familiarly known, had been previously convicted, and had served a short "stretch" in the county jail for a similar offense before. He denounced his arrest and conviction at this time, stating that he was being persecuted rather than prosecuted, because it was claimed he had threatened some of the officials in case he was apprehended. This he vehemently denied in court, and at the same time loudly protested that he was being made a mark while scores of others were not disturbed. Court officials who heard DeCaro's declaration were rather skeptical as to his ability to "catch on" either as a state or federal agent, but admitted that, because of his knowledge of the local "bootlegging" situation, he could, if he saw fit to do so, make some interesting disclosures on the conditions that prevail here.

In a moment of presumed levity, the Thompsonville Press printed the following on the front page of the March 4 issue.

Following his conviction for "bootlegging" in the Enfield Town Court last Saturday morning, Nicholas De Caro of Pleasant Street startled the court officials and attendants who were within his hearing with the following declaration:

"I'll take my medicine and serve my time, but when I get out, I will return here as a state cop or a federal agent and clean up the town."

"Nick" as he is familiarly known, had previously been convicted, and had served a short "stretch" in the county jail for a similar offense before. He denounced his arrest and conviction at this time, stating that he was being persecuted rather than prosecuted, because it was claimed that he had threatened some of the officials in the case [for which] he was apprehended.

When released he returned to town a minor goodfella.

On December 26, 1928, Carlo De Caro Sr. was notified that his request for naturalization had been denied based on a lack of character due to selling liquor during prohibition. He was told he could reapply in the future.

In December of 1929, as Frank H. Abbe and his wife of Enfield Street left for their annual winter sojourn to Florida, the senior De Caro notified police that someone had broken into his store at 22 Pleasant Street and had stolen two slot machines.

The fruit of two opposing lifestyles.

On September 24, 1931, Carlo De Caro finally became a naturalized citizen, having reapplied for reconsideration in February of 1929. Perhaps his record was clean by then, or the standards for naturalization had been lowered.

Over the next the years the De Caro's, Louie, Nicholas, and Carlo, seemed to have found peace in Thompsonville, either due to increased oversight by the local police force, or simply because they found new outlets for their energies, having become members in good standing with the Sons of Italy, acting on committees for Red Cross drives, and having engaged in the annual Mount Carmel Feast festivities.

Perhaps their collective change in demeanor was the maturing of the next generation of De Caro's as the offspring excelled in school, were recognized for their good works by the Italian American Society, and even joined social groups like the Boys Club and Foresters of America.

In 1940 Carlo De Caro even applied for a Tavern Permit with the State Liquor Control Commission so he could legally sell libations at his business at 17 Pleasant Street in Thompsonville.[127]

Times had certainly changed.

In early 1941 brother Nicholas De Carlo fell ill, unable to perform his duties as the President of Court Cavour, Foresters of America. By October of the same year Nicolas had recovered sufficiently to resume his duties. Brother Louie had assumed the post of secretary for the association in the interim.

But situations change quickly, and on Saturday, November 15th, Nicholas passed away after a recurrence of the earlier illness.

> *Mr. DeCaro was a native of Italy, but resided here since coming to this country 45 years ago. He was prominent in local Italian circles, and was president of a local Court of the Foresters of America. For 20 years Mr. DeCaro was proprietor of a barber shop in Springfield.[128]*

In 1942 the sons of Carlo De Caro, Mario, Raymond, and Ronald De Caro joined the service awaiting deployment, with Carlo Jr., at 18 years of age, only recently having registered for the draft. Louis De Caro's son Anthony, a pharmacist's mate, had already been stationed in Casablanca.

The De Caro family was well represented in the military,

---

[127] Thompsonville Press June 13, 1940. Page 7.
[128] Thompsonville Press November 20, 1041. Page 2.

as was the Bonelli family with Joseph Bonelli, son of Salvatore, in the Army stationed in Europe.

Carlo Jr. though, unlike his siblings, would never get the chance to serve his country, and surprisingly it wasn't due to his size, even though the young man of 19 years of age was clinically obese, tipping the scales at over 300 pounds which had led to his deferred draft classification.

By strange circumstances, fate had thrown young De Caro, 19, and the older Bonelli, 61, together, as both were employed by the Somersville Manufacturing Company and lived one block away from each other.

On work mornings the younger De Caro would leave his father's home at 71 Park Avenue, turn left on Summer Street and left again on Belmont, picking Bonelli up at his home at 31 Belmont Avenue. The two would take Elm Street traveling east to 21 North Street where De Caro would stop once again to pick up fellow employee Sylvester J. Richard before connecting to Hazard Avenue to complete the 6-mile trek to the manufactory.

Friday, September 24, 1943, was payday at the plant, and, as usual, De Caro dropped both Richards and Bonelli off at their respective homes in the afternoon. As Richards exited the vehicle De Caro told Richards to take the 6:30 am bus from Thompsonville to get to work the next day.

As he left Bonelli's house De Caro traveled 10 miles north to see his girlfriend, Eleanor Lawler of 46 Hastings Street, Springfield, Massachusetts, to borrow $20. It had been too late in the day to cash his paycheck and she was more than willing to loan De Caro the money, which he said he would pay back the following evening.

Completing the visit and the transaction, De Caro headed south from Lawler's residence to the home of Edmond Wasco, 16, who lived at 229 Enfield Street in

Thompsonville. De Caro had been badgering Wasco for days on end attempting to borrow or purchase a revolver from the lad, ostensibly for a friend who was headed to Maine that weekend to hunt. Wasco attended Enfield High School and was known to have a selection of armaments as he was a member of the State Guard Reserve and often practiced at the local Rifle Club range.

Reluctantly Wasco broke down and sold De Caro a handgun and a handful of long and short 22 caliber bullets for 15 dollars. De Caro smiled, as he was already 5 dollars to the good.

The next morning was Saturday, in previous years a day to celebrate by languishing in bed, but as the country was at war it was a normal workday. De Caro began the day as the previous, except that he found himself anxious and strangely excited at the same time, the forged steel in his jacket pocket weighing against his massive frame.

When De Caro was anxious, he ate, and his bulk indicated that he was anxious a good deal of the time.

As they headed out along Elm Street the young man suggested they stop to pick up coffee and some snacks to hold them over until they arrived in Somersville. Bonelli was in no mood to argue, and truth be told could have used some warm brew to help ease the hangover lingering from the evening before.

The purchase completed, the pair headed east again, but De Caro unexpectedly took a quick exit off Elm Street, just past the Kasperzak farm where local boys Bernard and Hugh Mackay and Joseph and Walter Kasperzak waited for a truck to take them to nearby tobacco fields for a day of work.

Driving up the unpaved road Bonelli was sure to have demanded an answer from the youth as to why he had gone off road.

But De Caro would have been in no mood to be questioned. He had never been in a position of power and the new emotion taking hold of him only emboldened him. He slammed on the brakes, bringing the car to a halt, the trailing dust from the road blanketing the automobile.

The overweight youth pulled the purchased gun from his jacket pocket and, turning quickly and gracefully for his size, emptied 6 shots into the startled Bonelli's head. The sound inside the car must have been deafening.

Calmly De Caro reloaded and fired one last shot into the passenger's chest, clearly savoring the moment.

Bonelli's brain cavity would have been emptied all over the passenger seat and door, and his blood would have covered the seat cover as he bled out.

De Caro would have been sprayed with bits of flesh and bone and blood from the bullets that had impacted the soft tissue and skull of Bonelli as he had twitched with each exploding bullet. It must have been exhilarating and terrifying at the same time for the obese teenager.

To consider the coldness required to empty the spent shells from the warm pistol, reload, and fire another round into the dead man's chest is almost beyond understanding.

And yet, De Caro had done what he had planned.

For a moment he must have sat there, overcome by taking the life of another man.

The power.

The control.

An act perhaps his siblings might never experience even though they were engaged in a world war overseas.

De Caro opened Bonelli's jacket to locate the man's

billfold, which he found, but it contained only a few dollars. A search of the dead man's trouser pockets proved more successful, as Bonelli carried his real money on a clip.

The youth counted out 1,508 dollars in bloodstained bills. Considering De Caro's weekly pay was 28 dollars per week it was the most money he had ever seen at one time ($34,000 in 2020).

He was rich.

His hands shook as adrenaline coursed through him.

When the exhilaration wore off mere moments later, the weight of his actions landed heavily on De Caro. A cold clammy terror wrapped around him, reaching inside his chest and wrapping its fingers around his heart.

Panic.

A new emotion.

Beyond anxiety and much more motivating.

He would have to bury the body and clean his car.

De Caro popped the trunk and pulled out a flat blade shovel he kept there for emergencies.

This clearly was one.

Flat bladed shovels are best used to move dirt, gravel, sand, and stone. In this instance its efficiency helped the struggling, sweating, and obese youth carve out a shallow grave on the side of the dirt road. It took several attempts before suitably loose ground was found.

De Caro dragged the body from his car, his breath coming in gulps as he was unused to that kind of labor. Sweat ran in rivulets down his forehead, stinging his eyes, and down his back as well, running between the folds of layered fat which covered his massive bulk.

He buried Bonelli quickly to hide the crime, dragging branches over the mounded dirt and gravel.

Satisfied, he threw the shovel into the trunk, slid back into his car, fired up the engine, and turned the car around, heading west along East Street.

Passing the Kaspersak place again, students Mary Kaspersak and Lillian Button, waiting for the school bus at the end of the driveway, noticed De Caro as he sped past, alone in the car, hunched over the wheel.

Abraham Sisisky, local chief observer of the Aircraft Warning System Corps and owner of the Enfield Motor Company at 917 Enfield Street usually opened his business at 8:00 in the morning. At 7:30 the place was empty, and De Caro wheeled into the lot, pulling up next to the tire tube test stand water tank. Pulling a rag off a nearby piece of equipment the portly youth did his best to wash Bonelli's blood and brains off the car passenger door, the flesh and fluid already clotting.

The effort was marginally successful.

When Sisisky arrived 20 minutes later, he was surprised to find a large amount of blood in the water tank as he emptied and refilled it. The bloody rag prompted him to call the police.

The seven gunshots, even muffled as they echoed inside the confines of the car, caught the attention of the four boys waiting for their ride on East Street, and, since the truck hadn't yet arrived, they decided to investigate the sound, taking off into the woods at a healthy trot.

The boys broke through the clearing sometime later onto a little used grass and dirt road east of the family farm.

Fresh tire tracks over matted grass drew their attention as they headed up the side road.

They came upon a fresh mound of dirt, and suspecting adventure they threw the brush aside and began to dig with discarded tin cans nearby. To their horror they uncovered a human body, still warm.

They ran home and their parents called the police.

Arriving at his home Carlo Jr. went inside, washed, changed his clothes, and called in sick to work.

What to do next?

De Caro surveyed his car. Grabbing a can of turpentine from the garage he set about scrubbing the passenger door and dashboard. Satisfied that the interior was passable, the teen realized the bloodstained passenger seat would have to be addressed next. He headed north to Springfield to the upholstery business of John H. Cote, where he purchased two new seat covers for the vehicle, explaining away the brown stains as an unfortunate result from rabbit hunting.

De Caro then drove over to Hastings Street to see Eleanor, to return the loaned money from the day before.

Did Carlo Jr. confess his actions to Lawler? She certainly noticed the new seat covers, money laying on the passenger seat, and the faint smell of kerosene in the car.

What might she have suspected?

Did she question him? Suggest a next action?

Whatever the case, De Caro left Lawler and drove the 3.5 miles south to Forest Park where he found a secluded spot and buried not only the stolen money but 13 sheets of counterfeit "A" class gasoline rationing coupons which he had purchased earlier.

At that point he most likely rested.

Back in Thompsonville events had been rapidly unfolding, beginning with the arrival of the Enfield Police at the shallow gravesite. At first, due to the brutal nature of the killing, disposal of the body, and history of the deceased, the detectives considered the murder a mob hit.

But Lieutenant Gene S. Lenzi and Hartford County detective pistol packin' Joseph F. Mitchell[129] weren't convinced after closely checking the man's acquaintances and movements that morning. The De Caro family background was known to the local police and officers found out that Carlo Jr. hadn't clocked into his regular Saturday shift.

An officer was posted outside the De Caro home to wait for the young man should he return.

And return he did from Forest Park early that afternoon and was taken into custody, the youth quickly breaking down and confessing to the murder and subsequent robbery of Salvatore Bonelli.

Within hours De Caro had made two unsuccessful suicide attempts.

Justice moved swiftly as De Caro was arraigned the Thursday following the murder of Bonelli, whose funeral was held on Tuesday, September 28, 1943, at the Browne Funeral Home on Pearl Street in Thompsonville.

Carlo J. De Caro Jr. was charged with the first degree slaying of his work partner and neighbor and was ordered held without bail until October 5th when the case against him would be presented to a Hartford Grand Jury.

---

[129] Vox-Cop Volume 2 Issue 11 1945. Page 2.

Must Die in Chair

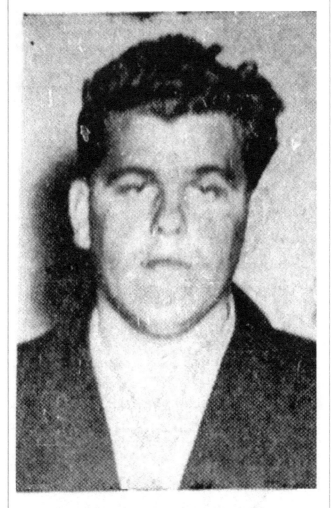

CARLOS J. DeCARO.

The Thompsonville youth was summarily indicted on two counts, the first being murder in the perpetration of a robbery, and the second willful, deliberate, and premeditated murder.

On October 29, De Caro was denied a sanity test by the court, States Attorney Hugh M. Alcorn, Jr. successfully arguing that the youth had already been examined by a state psychologist and found sane and competent.

By December 2nd jurors had been selected from the surrounding towns, including six women and six men.

The following day the state began its prosecution, and by Wednesday, December 16, 1943, De Caro had been found guilty on the charge of first-degree murder after less than three hours of deliberation.

Under state law Superior Court Judge William H. Comely had no alternative but to sentence De Caro to death by electrocution, the date set at May 3 of the following year.

On April 25, 1944. De Caro's request for a stay of execution was rejected by the State Board of Pardons.

On May 3, 1944, at 10:05:20 p.m. Carlo James De Caro Jr. entered the death chamber accompanied by a prison guard on his right and the prison chaplain on his left.

It took less than a minute to strap the youth in, although his size and weight tested the strength and structure of the wooden chair.

The first of five charges of electricity was given at 10:02:45 with a final charge at 10:05:40.

The youth was declared dead at 10:07 p.m.

Unlike Kemmler, De Caro did not come back to life.

Connecticut had perfected execution by electrocution by that time, as De Caro was the seventh person to die in the electric chair since the state had abolished the more entertaining death by hanging in 1936.

Somewhere Edison was smiling.

9: UPPITY

The house on 2.5 acres known as *The Beeches* was sold to Mr. and Mrs. Donald Nelson Lanz of Somers in July of 1953 for $35,000 [$400,000 in 2020 dollars], ending the 12-year Enfield residency of Paul Robeson and family.

The Lanz's were an upper-class white family, Donald employed in the experimental engineering department of Pratt & Whitney Aircraft in East Hartford. He was a member in good standing in Fayette Lodge #69, Ancient Free and Accepted Masons of the Masonic Lodge in Ellington, Connecticut.

His wife, Helen, was regaled as an outstanding roller skater throughout New England, the sport seeming to be an acceptable outlet for women at the time.[130]

The purchase of the property by a freemason and his roller-skating wife was most likely a breath of fresh air for the region, helping to salve the dishonor brought upon the community after the House [on] Un-American Activities Committee (HUAC) had labeled Robeson a Communist based upon his years of working for the rights of black men

---

[130] Thompsonville Press July 23, 1953. Page 5.

in America and all over the world.

Robeson wasn't only a fine singer and entertainer, but an opinionated and well-spoken black man.

Some may say uppity.

Paul Leroy Robeson was born on April 9, 1898, in Princeton, New Jersey. His father was a Presbyterian minister and his mother a Quaker.

His early years were anything but easy, as his father resigned his ministry in 1901 due to a disagreement with the white financial supporters of the church.[131]

When Robeson turned six his mother, nearly blind at the time, died in a house fire.[132]

Finances became more difficult, and the family moved into an attic apartment in Westfield, New Jersey.[133]

Finally in 1910 Robeson's father found stable employment at the St. Thomas A.M.E. Zion Church in Somerville, N.J.[134] Robeson attended Somerville High School where he not only excelled in football, basketball, baseball, and track, but also sang in the school chorus and acted in school performances.

Prior to graduation and being named class valedictorian, he entered and won a statewide academic contest for a scholarship to Rutgers University. He was the third black

---

[131] Duberman 1989, pp. 6–7; cf. Robeson 2001, pp. 5–6, Boyle & Bunie 2005, pp. 18–20

[132] Boyle & Bunie 2005, pp. 22–23; cf. Duberman 1989, p. 8, Robeson 2001, pp. 7–8

[133] Robeson 2001, p. 11; cf. Duberman 1989, p. 9, Boyle & Bunie 2005, pp. 27–29

[134] Duberman 1989, pp. 9–10; cf. Brown 1997, p. 39, Robeson 2001, pp. 13–14

student that had ever been enrolled at Rutgers and was the only one at the time.

Race was always present, no matter his athletic, vocal, or educational prowess.

He could only sing informally on-campus with the Glee Club as membership required attending all-white mixers.

As a sophomore he was benched when a Southern football team, Washington and Lee University, refused to take the field because Rutgers had fielded a black student.

In his junior year his father passed away, never getting a chance to marvel at his son's collegiate accomplishments.

He finished college with varsity letters in multiple sports, and his success in football won him first-team All-American selection in both his junior and senior years, with Walter Camp considering him to be the greatest end ever. He was accepted into Phi Beta Kappa, Cap and Skull, and finished his education as class valedictorian. In his valedictory speech, he exhorted his classmates to work for equality for all Americans.

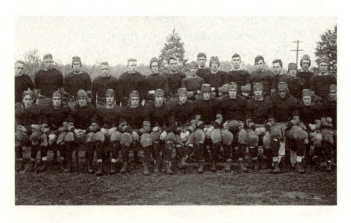

Rutgers football team 1918. Robeson is the only black player.

If these achievements weren't enough, he was regionally recognized for his deep rich baritone voice, a talent on which he would rely for greater fame later in life.

As a postgraduate Robeson entered New York University School of Law in the Fall of 1919. Uncomfortable at NYU, he soon moved to Harlem and transferred to Columbia Law School in February 1920. While in school Robeson played professional football for both the Akron Pros and the Milwaukee Badgers of the National Football League.

He graduated from Columbia Law School in 1923.

Robeson worked briefly as a lawyer, but once again institutional racism caused him to quit the profession,[135] and he immersed himself in acting, quickly landing high profile roles which attracted national attention.

From that point on Robeson career skyrocketed on both sides of the Atlantic, with the actor purchasing a home in England as he performed extensively there. London was far more accepting of performers of color, and Robeson took to Great Britain as well.

Robeson recorded songs at Abbey Road Studios, performed on Broadway, in London, and acted in films. In 1938 he was named by American Motion Picture Herald as the 10th most popular star in British cinema.

It was during the period of 1937 to 1939 when Robeson found his voice on political issues, particularly when voicing his concerns about Fascism. By the beginning of World War Two he had been targeted for arrest by Germany, which may or may not have influenced his decision to return to the United States in 1940.

---

[135] Boyle & Bunie 2005, pp. 111–14; cf. Duberman 1989, pp. 54–55, Robeson 2001, pp. 71–72

Paul and Eslanda Robeson with their son Paul Jr., Enfield, c. 1950. Reprinted with permission of Connecticut Historical Society.

During a promotional tour in 1940, the Beverly Wilshire Hotel was the only major Los Angeles hotel willing to accommodate Robeson due to his race, and even then, he was charged an exorbitant rate.

He registered under an assumed name and dedicated two hours every afternoon to sitting in the lobby, where he was widely recognized, to silently shame the California hotel. Based on his actions Los Angeles hotels lifted their restrictions on black guests shortly afterwards.

On April 1, 1941, in a wry coincidence April Fool's Day, multiple regional newspapers reported the purchase of the Thompsonville, Connecticut, property known as The Beeches by, as The Meriden Daily Journal's headline noted:

Paul Robeson, Negro Actor, Buys Estate.

The Journal went on to recount the current state of disrepair of the property, and that it housed its own bowling alley, and an outdoor swimming pool.

The Hartford Courant was more delicate in reporting on the transaction, with not even a mention of the actor/singer's race. They chose instead to extol the virtues of the property and that repairs were underway, with a hope of imminent occupancy.

His attorney did inform the paper that the Robeson's had selected Thompsonville due to the fact they had long admired this area of Connecticut and were taken with the beauty of the colonial home.

On April 3, 1941, the Thompsonville Press weekly reported on the event as well, although the article was either cribbed directly from the Meriden paper, or possibly from some press release that contained similar information.

In the same paper, taking a prominent position above the fold, a report noted, in a nod to April Fool's Day, that Robeson had called Mayor Cornelius Sullivan's office and conducted a lengthy conversation with the elected official. That call was followed up with another one to the Town Clerk Francis Olschafskie which concluded with the clerk inviting Mr. Robeson to lunch at 1:15 that same day.

When Mr. Robeson failed to show two hours past the

scheduled time, the officials realized they had been duped.

On June 18, 1941, the famous singer made a surprise appearance at the Class Day exercises at Enfield High School. It was Robeson's first public appearance since purchasing his Enfield home, and the visit was arranged between Everett King, who was the contractor in charge of repairs for the singer's property, and his daughter, Margaret King, who was chairperson for the day's activities.

After an introduction by the school principal Karl Lee, the performer sang four songs for the audience, including a stirring rendition of "Ole Man River."

In September a Thompsonville Press reporter conducted a sympathetic interview with the performer. Excerpts follow and reflect the character of the man, providing insights as well.

Paul Robeson, Singer of Note, Assumes Role as Commentator

Distinguished Soloist and Actor Sets Forth His Views on Art and Other Subjects in Interview at Enfield Residence – Has Taken Stump As An Anti-Fascist Both Here And Abroad

You can have the voice, the smile, and the acting ability to win stardom, he says, but if you're going to be a real artist of the people, you've got to have social consciousness as well.

...from this social consciousness stems a quality which permits Welsh miners, seeing him on the street as they did for the first time in 1925, to call out, as if they were old friends "Hello Paul".

Millions of others have seen Paul Robeson only from

one side of the footlights but feel as if they know him too.

The answer is that Robeson, whose father was a slave and whose mother was a schoolteacher, sings their songs, talks their language, is one of them.

"Soon after I made my debut in England in 1925, I began to wonder why I had been able to capture the sympathy of the Welsh miners and the English workingman. I came conclusion that they had felt close to me because I am a Negro, a member of a race that is being kicked around.

It made me realize that I, as a Negro, was not the only person that was suffering, that the problems of the Negro were the problems of the workingman generally.

It became further clear to me that the fight of the English working people against Fascism was my fight too, and I worked and I sang for the loyalist Spain, and I took the platform with Sir Stanford Cripp (Britain's present [then] ambassador to Soviet Russia). George Bernard Shaw and others were advocating a pact between Britain and Russia."

Robeson visited the Soviet Union for the first time in 1934 and went back every year thereafter until 1938.

"The high morale of the Russians is due in large part to the fact that racial differences in the Soviet Union have been eliminated." [136]

The article ended with a short personal history of Robeson, his acting and singing triumphs, and ended with a

---

[136] Thompsonville Press September 4, 1941. Page 3.

summary of his physical appearance, as if his personal beliefs hadn't been enough to enhance his stature.

All in all, it was a well-balanced article.

On March 27, 1941, Robeson delivered what was the first of his annual concerts on behalf of the Enfield Teachers' Association in the local High School Auditorium. Appearing with the performer was a native concert pianist of Enfield, Donald M. Comrie, who attended the Brooklyn Academy of Music, Julliard, and had a distinguished professional career.

Four months later Robeson wrapped up his performance in *Emperor Jones* at the Ivoryton, Connecticut, Playhouse to rave reviews.

> *Hearing bravos! Which we have never heard at a summer theatre…Listening to the crowd's ooh-and-ah about Robeson's sterling performance. Everyone seems pleased at having been there.*
>
> *Then for a minute with the great – and we mean great – Paul…Dressed in sweatshirt and old trousers…Ready to ride to Enfield…All smiles, as always…talks about his "understanding wife" and his son…Says he first played the Emperor role in Provincetown.*
>
> *In fact that was where he got his start. It was in 1924 and into the role he whistled, then hummed a bit…The audience asked for more…Today you have Robeson, a man with a most dynamic, robust, flaring personality and of course, a great and glorious voice!* [137]

---

[137] Hartford Courant July 23, 1941. Page 7.

Following the Japanese bombing of Pearl Harbor naval base in 1941, the U.S. entered World War II on the side of the allies. Every able-bodied American male was drafted to fight overseas.

As a result, the U.S. Maritime Commission had to find workers to produce large numbers of Victory Ships and Liberty Ships for the war effort.

Paul Robeson sings to laborers working at the racially integrated Moore shipyards in Oakland, California. September 21, 1942. Property of Oakland Tribune.

On the West Coast, Moore Dry Dock Shipyards in Oakland and Kaiser Shipyards in Richmond, California became national centers for round-the-clock wartime production. The widespread opposition to hiring either minorities or women workers that had existed at the beginning of the war had been addressed by President Franklin Roosevelt's with executive order 8802, which banned all forms of racial discrimination in defense work.

On September 21, 1942, Robeson visited the brotherhood of builders at their shipyard to celebrate the efforts of all involved.

In 1942 Robeson narrated the documentary *Native Land* which was labeled by the FBI as communist propaganda. The independently produced film depicted the struggle of trade unions against union-busting corporations, their spies, and contractors. It was based on the 1938 report of the La Follette Committee's investigation of the repression of labor organizing.

It wouldn't be the last time the government would try to associate Robeson with the dreaded "communism".

Like clockwork, Robeson once again performed at Enfield High School in support of the Teachers' Association on May 28, 1943, his second annual concert in his adopted hometown.

Four days later the singer was awarded an honorary degree from Morehouse College in Atlanta, Georgia.

More honors kept coming for Robeson the following year, as:

- He was presented an award from the National Federation for Constitutional Liberties for his outstanding contribution toward ending racial discrimination in our country and tyranny and oppression throughout the world.
- On his 46th birthday at the 17th regiment Armory in New York City he was revered by the Council

on African affairs and serenaded by the likes of jimmy Durante, Count Basie, Duke Ellington, and Hazel Scott.

- He received an award from the American Academy of Arts and Letters
- He received a citation from The Sign, a national Catholic religious publication
- He was awarded the Spingarn Medal from the National Association for the Advancement of Colored People

For two years the performer toured North America performing Othello, first performing the role at the Shubert Theatre in New York City in 1943, becoming the first African American to play the role with a white supporting cast on Broadway. During the same period, he petitioned the commissioner of baseball, as well as many owners, to integrate Major League Baseball.

His efforts were rebuffed.

Returning to Enfield after a long multiyear national tour, Robeson performed his third concert under the sponsorship of the Enfield Teachers' Association on June 22, 1946. Accompanying the singer was William Schatzkamer, a concert pianist from New York, who had played at the 1943 high school concert as well.

The Hartford Times drama critic reviewed Robeson's performance.

> *Three years ago Paul Robeson, having found a rooftree in Enfield consented generously to give a concert (and this time the word give means just that) for the benefit of the child health program of the Enfield Teacher's Association. It is now called the Paul Robeson Child Welfare Fund and the project seems to have become an annual affair.*

Saturday night in Enfield High School Mr. Robeson sang his third concert for the hometown people and although he had only just returned from one of the most strenuous tours of his career he appeared to enjoy it as a real homecoming.

He brough with him his regular accompanist, Lawrence Brown, and the assisting pianist who appeared with him in Hartford, William Schatzkamer. So it was a Robeson concert in all respects and more too because, as a final encore, he turned actor and gave the closing speech of Othello. He sang all those indicative songs by which we know that what Robeson believes he sings, and what he sings he believes.

The applause rang through the pack gym-auditorium was of hair-trigger spontaneity and of rolling enthusiasm no matter what he sang. He was a great artist giving all he had; a great fellow townsman come home.[138]

Meanwhile, further south, Paul Robeson, Jr. was completing basic training at the AAF Military Training Center in San Antonio, Texas. Young Robeson's military participation reflected the family's commitment to the country and demonstrated their belief in American ideals.

On July 25, 1946, two married black couples, George W. and Mae Murray Dorsey, and Roger and Dorothy Malcom, were murdered on a dirt road by a mob of white men in Walton and Oconee counties between Monroe and

---

[138] Hartford Times article reprinted in Thompsonville Press June 27, 1946. Page 1.

Watkinsville, Georgia. It was referred to as the Moore's Ford lynching, even though the actual assault occurred elsewhere, the cited location simply afforded an easily identifiable place in a remote area.

It's important to understand that lynching is defined as the public killing of an individual who has not received any due process and is not limited to hanging.

Horrified, Robeson announced the formation of **An American Crusade to End Lynching** on September 14, 1946. National celebrities, intellectuals, and educators such as Albert Einstein, Joe Louis, Frank Sinatra, Orson Welles, and Lena Horne signed on to the effort. Robeson called for a National Pilgrimage to Washington on September 23 in support of the effort and northern cities like Boston, Chicago, Detroit prepared delegations to march on the capital.

The three-point action program proposed by Robeson included the:

- Apprehension and punishment of every lyncher
- Passage of a federal anti-lynching bill, and
- Refusal to seat Ku Klux Klan members in Congress.

Robeson and a smaller delegation met with President Truman to push their agenda, and Truman pushed back. While Truman stated that America and Great Britain were the last refuge of freedom in the world, Robeson countered that the British Empire had been one of the greatest enslavers of all mankind, and Southern lynchings did not reflect good will to all mankind.

Truman viewed the lynching "issue" as a problem with political timing, while Robeson quite rightly viewed it as an issue of survival.

After the meeting a reporter brought up the possibility of Robeson being a communist, which the actor refuted. A narrative was beginning to be constructed as the media took their direction from a government caught in Robeson's social justice crosshairs.

It seemed that any black American who was educated and had a valid opinion on a subject that either put the government or society at large in a questionable spotlight drew both the attention and ire of that same government. Robeson certainly did, as did William Edward Burghardt Du Bois who had completed his graduate work at the Friedrich Wilhelm University (in Berlin, Germany) and at Harvard University, where he was the first black man to earn a doctorate. He was a professor of history, sociology, and economics at Atlanta University and had co-founded the National Association for the Advancement of Colored People (NAACP) in 1909.

Uppity….but educated.

In considering the aftermath of the Robeson Truman meeting the Hartford Chronicle, surprisingly, came to the actor's defense.

> *People of Paul Robeson's calibre [sic caliber] do not excite easily. They can usually practice moderation and patience to an amazing degree. And when they let it go it is as much through fear as it is anger.*
>
> *We suspect that Paul Robeson is as excited as many others of us by the bitter desperation within the group; a desperation that is generating an ominous sort of hate for a savage sort of whiteness.*
>
> *There is too much open, cold blooded murder of citizens on the highways in broad daylight; too much ignoring of permanent mutilation of defenseless individuals; too much deliberate smashing of hokes and intimidation of people who merely want a chance to live.*

Maybe Paul Robeson's remarks to President Truman did have an element of threat to them, but the greatest threat involved really is the threat to all Democracy involved in a nation's indifference to internal atrocities – while it condemns the same thing in others thousands of miles away.[139]

Still, the government was not to be swayed from its efforts to paint Robeson a communist. The day after the Hartford article appeared, Robeson found himself testifying in front of the California Senate Factfinding Subcommittee on Un-American Activities. Senator Jack Breckinridge Tenney, chairman of the committee, asked Robeson directly, on the record, "Are you a Communist?"

Robeson once again denied that he was.

But Tenney was simply playing his part in a grand scheme defined as the Illusory Truth Effect, which states *we tend to believe something is true after being exposed to it multiple times.* The more times we hear something, the truer it seems. The effect is so powerful that repetition can persuade anyone to believe information known to be false is true.

By January of the following year Robeson announced that he would be abandoning the theater and the concert stages to focus on his work against racial hatred and prejudice.

By April 1947, Robeson had been named by the House Committee on Un-American Activities as one of a group of persons "invariably found supporting the Communist Party

---

[139] Hartford Chronicle Saturday October 5, 1946. Page 6.

and its front organization."[140]

That same month, on April 19, Robeson was denied the use of a small assembly hall in Peoria, Illinois, for a benefit concert. The actor stated that the town had been taken over by a Fascist element. The town responded that they were afraid his performance would cause unrest.

Six days later Robeson was barred from performing at the Philip Schuyler High School auditorium in upstate New York as the Mayor of the town, Erastus Corning, objected to holding a function of a highly controversial nature in a school building.[141]

Robeson pushed back through the courts, and the State Supreme Court ruled in his favor "even though the court believed him to be a communist."[142] The Robeson concert went forward.

Of little interest at the time was the inclusion at the end of the Meriden Daily Journal article that:

(Robeson's home is in Enfield.) [143]

The little town bordering Massachusetts was tainted, no longer noted and admired for hosting a great singer and actor, but for harboring a Communist.

It had only been two years since the surrender of Nazi Germany in 1945, but the uneasy alliance between the United States and the Soviet Union had quickly turned to distrust with March 12, 1947, identified as the beginning of the Cold War between the nations.

---

[140] The Meriden Daily Journal April 19, 1947. Page 10.

[141] Hartford Courant April 25, 1947. Page 2.

[142] Hartford Courant May 7, 1947. Page 17.

[143] Hartford Courant May 7, 1947. Page 17.

Now one word – communist – could not only strike fear into the hearts of Americans but would be repurposed to color the reputations of intellectuals and performers, and even draw the entire nation into conflicts of suspect nature in later years.

The media played its role in selectively identifying individuals and assisting in making them social pariahs, as if they were the carriers of some horrific communicable disease instead of people who sought social change and modifications in policies for the disadvantaged.

Commie.

Fellow Traveler.

Red.

It had been a government directed assault on the character of Paul Robeson as soon as he spoke his mind about the lynchings of blacks in the South in the heated meeting with President Harry S. Truman.

If he had only "stayed in his lane" and not gotten involved in calling out the government for its implicit approval of white southerners murdering black citizens.

But no.

Robeson had to speak up, and the government and media had to shut him down.

Through the following years no paper was more caustic in its reporting on Robeson than the Meriden Daily Journal, mostly through its republication of King Features Syndicate's opinion columnist George Sokolsky. Sokolsky was a rabid nationalist and took every opportunity to question and take Robeson to task for his views and opinions.[144]

Robeson fervently opposed the Mundt-Nixon bill, named after Karl E. Mundt and Richard Nixon. The proposed legislation was formally known as the Subversive Activities Control Act, which would have required all members of the Communist Party of the United States register with the Attorney General. The bill passed the House 319-58, but failed in the Senate, not by vote, simply due to inaction.

While Congress was focused on Mundt-Nixon it held up discussion of an anti-lynching bill which had been proposed by Hubert Humphrey, Senator of Minnesota, and, surprisingly, backed by President Harry Truman.

In an opinion column in its June 2, 1948, edition, the Meriden Daily Journal went so far as to suggest that Robeson simply go back to Russia.

The best solution to his problems, it would seem, might be found in a permanent residence in Russia. He would be missed from the musical world, but, as a citizen, his absence would leave no important gap. For he has chosen to take the wrong road toward the betterment of conditions under democracy. He has lent encouragement and support to those who seek to undermine the government under which we live. Under the circumstances, we could spare him if Russia wants to take him in. By his own assertion, he feels more at home in the shadow of the Kremlin than on American soil. [145]

---

[144] Meriden Daily Journal May 4, 1948. Page 6. June 1, 1948. Page 1. June 2, 1948. Page 6. June 5, 1948. Page 6. Feb 15, 1949. Page 6.

[145] Meriden Daily Journal June 2, 1948. Page 6.

The ***Chronicle and Comment*** opinion section of the December 12, 1948, edition of the Thompsonville Press took Robeson to the woodshed.

Yale is a great University.

Connecticut is a great state.

Both of these institutions were made greater and finer and better by the election of Levi Jackson as Captain of the Yale Varsity football squad.

Levi Jackson is a colored boy.

He was elected unanimously.

All of this is good for Yale, Connecticut, and the United States of America.

We commend this action to Paul Robeson, the distinguished artist, who is a resident of this community. Perhaps he will have more Faith in people not of his racial origin. [146]

It seemed that, in the opinion of the writer, the election of a black athlete as captain of a university football squad counterbalanced the unchecked murders of black men, women, and children all over the country, as well as the subtle fascism of the American government as it sought to regulate the inalienable right to free speech and activities of its citizenry.

By August 10, 1950, the Thompsonville Press opinion piece clarified the position of the Enfield community-at-large concerning Paul Robeson.

---

[146] Thompsonville press December 12, 1948. Page 1.

If Robeson had simply stuck to singing and entertaining, he could have remained a respected member of the community, but as soon as he began to work and speak on behalf of people of color, well, a line had been crossed, and a little bit of a *Southern attitude* crept into the Thompsonville newspaper.

> *Paul Robeson is a fine singer, and a man of wildly distorted views on politics. As time goes by, his singing voice is more and more eclipsed by one he uses in his diatribes against the United States, and his adulation of the Soviet Union.*
>
> *Mr. Robeson has enjoyed a many good advantages in the United States. He was well-educated here, he became an outstanding athlete while in college, and later attained success and fame as a singer and actor. You might think he would be impressed with the opportunity the United States offers to those willing to work for it, and to recognize it when it comes.*
>
> *His reaction, however, was the opposite. Instead of becoming, like Jackie Robinson, and many other of his race who has fought his way to the top by sheer ability, a champion of the American way of life, he became one of its most virulent critics. Bit by bit, he became a crusader for the Soviet Union, forsaking the concert hall for the political platform.*
>
> *His misguided enthusiasm for the Russian way of doing things took him all around the world, where he capitalized on the fame his singing had brought him in this country. But now the State Department feels he has gone too far in his campaign of denunciation against the nation that gave him his opportunity. It demands that he surrender his passport. He refuses to give it up.*

It is not a pleasant thing, the tragedy of Paul Robeson. It is depressing to think how much more he might have made of his life and his talent had he devoted himself as wholeheartedly to improving and strengthening America as he has to indiscriminately attacking her. But what can anyone think of a native-born American who only last month was demanding publicly that we keep our hands off Korea?

So the order has gone out to stop him if he tries to leave. It is an unusual fate for a native-born American to be thus imprisoned in his country, but Paul Robeson has only himself to blame for it. [147]

Shades of Cassius Clay [Muhammad Ali], John Lennon, Jane Fonda, Edward Snowden, and others.

The article left Robeson no real choice but to leave the community that he had adopted years earlier.

The same local newspaper that had lauded the arrival of the singer, the same community that had accepted and attended his performances on behalf of the Teachers Union, had thrown the last handful of dirt on his grave.

Less opinion, more singing....

You're only as free as we let you be.

---

[147] Thompsonville Press August 10, 1950. Page 1. Opinion.

10: PACIFIC FLYER

The birthplace of Thomas James Ash Sr. is in question, as only his christening record is available. That document identifies the location of that event as St. Chad, Birmingham, Warwickshire, England. The US Census of 1900 agrees, but the Census of 1930 does not, identifying his birthplace as in the Irish Free State. His birth date of May 26, 1853, is not in question.

His wife, Mary Elizabeth Wright, has a similar complicated history with her certificate citing Southampton, Burlington, New Jersey as her place of birth. The US Census of 1930 disagrees, identifying England as her country of birth instead. Her birthdate of October 10, 1860, seems secure.

According to the 1920 US Census, Thomas Ash Sr. emigrated to the United States with his parents Patrick Ash, wife Mary Fitzpatrick Ash, and their family one year after his birth, in 1854. As one might expect, the 1930 Census contradicts that date and instead identifies 1857 as the year of emigration. If that wasn't enough confusion, the 1900 census cites 1860 as the year of emigration of the family.

With the arrival dates so contradictory, the best that can

be determined is that the Ash family initially put down roots in Passaic, New Jersey based on the 1880 Federal Census.

That same record identifies the father Patrick being employed as a general contracted painter. Son Thomas Sr. worked as a machinist alongside his brothers, Christopher, and William, each employed at the Calico Print Works.

Passaic (Calico) Print Works textile manufacturing.

By 1900, twenty years later, the core of the family had relocated to Worcester, Massachusetts, the move being preceded by the death of son Christopher.

After their arrival in the Bay State, in a sequence of sad events, Patrick's wife Mary Fitzpatrick died in 1900, daughter Mary in 1901, and Patrick himself in 1903.

Thomas Sr. and his wife Elizabeth had not joined his parents, opting to remain behind, relocating to Yonkers, Westchester, New York in the early 1880s where their five children were born. Thomas Sr. was still making his living as a machinist, his skills easily transferable in an Industrial Age. The oldest daughter Emily was neither married nor employed. Mary, Thomas Jr., and Hazel were enrolled in school, and infant son William was at home with his mother.

After his father's death Thomas Sr. moved north as well, purchasing a small farm in Enfield, beginning employment as a master mechanic at the Hartford Carpet Corporation in Thompsonville, Connecticut. The family had certainly settled in the area by April 13, 1905, as it was reported in that day's edition of the Thompsonville Press that young Thomas Ashe [sic Ash] Jr. had suffered a broken leg when falling from an overturned play wagon while riding down a hill, presumably near his home.

Thomas Ash Jr (far right) and siblings circa 1908 (property of Holly Samociuk – used with permission)

Ash Jr. had certainly recovered well enough by late July of 1907 to participate in the first ever field event held by the Enfield Athletic Association on grounds owned by the group near his family farm. Not only did the youth participate, but he won the event with a 23-point total score, with the next closest competitor, Ned Allen, coming in at 16 points.

The number of events at the competition was limited, but interest was high, and the affair was well attended by locals. Some of the sports events were unusual, such as a wheelbarrow race, which Ash Jr. and George McAllister won, while others were more traditional, like the standing broad jump, pole vault, hop-step-jump, high jump, 100-yard dash, and shot put.[148]

By 1909 Ash Jr was enrolled in high school and was competing in school sponsored events as a member of the Enfield High School track team under the tutelage of Herbert Prentice. Thomas was proving to be quite good at certain events as demonstrated in first place finishes in the broad jump, high jump, and pole vault in a competition against athletes from Derby High School.[149]

Thomas continued his victories the following year, placing first again in the running hop-step-jump, pole vault, running high jump, and broad jump. The lad certainly had a spring in his step.

Not only was Ash Jr. successful on the field, but he excelled in his studies as well, and was an executive member of the High School Debating Society.[150]

By July of 1914 the United States was engaged in World War One, and two years later, at the age of 22, Thomas elected to attend a military training camp in Plattsburgh, New York over the summer of 1916, joining over 500 youths from Connecticut who participated in the exercises.

Looking to support the war effort, Ash Jr. was working cleaning cotton for munitions at the Nashua River Paper Company in East Pepperell, Massachusetts, 105 miles northeast of the family home.

---

[148] Thompsonville Press July 18 & July 25, 1907. Page 2.

[149] Thompsonville Press April 29, 1909. Page 4.

[150] Hartford Courant April1 1, 1911. Page 18.

The Nashua River Paper Company. (Nashua River Watershed Association, from the postcard collection of Elizabeth Ainsley Campbell.)

While working and living there, Thomas, 24 years old and single, registered for the draft on June 17th, 1917.

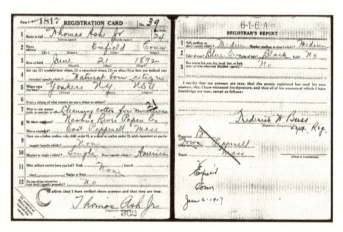

One month later, on July 13, 1917, Thomas Ash Jr. had enlisted in the Army Air Service. By August 9th he had entered a new Ground School Program that had been established at the Massachusetts Institute of Technology

(MIT) for training student officers.

The Secretary of the Navy had established the first ground school for pilot training at MIT only weeks before Ash's enlistment. The first class of fifty student pilots had arrived on July 23, 1917, for an eight-week training program covering electricity, signals, photography, seamanship, navigation, gunnery, aeronautic engines, theory of flight, and aircraft instruments.

New classes arrived at intervals of two weeks which meant that Thomas Ash Jr. was included in the second group of recruits to the program.

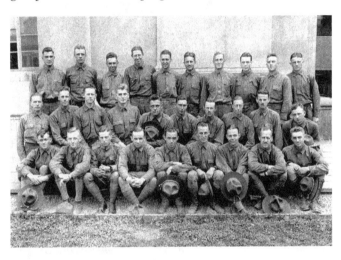

M.I.T. School of Military Aeronautics, Squadron F. (Payden Collection Yale School of 1918).

The last of 34 classes graduated two and a half years later on January 18, 1919. Of the 4,911 students enrolled in the ground school over the years, 3,622 graduated qualified for preliminary flight training.[151]

---

[151] Van Wyen. Naval Aviation in World War 1. Pgs 16-20 & 80.

By October 27, 1917, Ash Jr. found himself onboard the S. S. Manchuria leaving the Port of Hoboken, New Jersey, headed for France where he would enter the Ecole Militaire d 'Aviation at Avord, Department of Cher, France.

Ecole Militaire d 'Aviation at Avord, Department of Cher, France

The French Military Aviation School was highly regarded and afforded new recruit's instruction in:

> *...air combat, in the dropping [of] bombs, and the use of heavy projectiles; how they are trained to fly at night and in the feats of acrobatism on which their lives may sometime depend...*[152]

Back home in Enfield, tragedy struck, as William Ash, Thomas's brother, passed away at the age of 20. The family posted a "Card of Thanks" to all who reached out to express

---

[152] New York Times Our Fliers Want French Training June 3, 1917. Page 32.

their sorrow through flowers, words, or deeds.

In the February 28, 1918, edition of the Thompsonville Press, the paper printed a letter it had received from Thomas Ash Jr., stationed at that time in France.

February 6, 1918

The Thompsonville Press,

Gentlemen, I wish to thank you sincerely for the copies of the Press I received last evening. They were doubly welcome, for, being attached to the French Army, I receive very little news of America, except that contained in my letters. I perused them with great pleasure, and eagerly look forward to the new ones, for I hope you will continue to send them.

Please change my address to that given below, for soon I'll join an esquadrille [French aircraft squadron] at the front, and will continually be on the move.

Thanking you again, please consider me yours,

Lt. Thomas Ash Jr.

American Expeditionary Force via Paris, France

One month later, on March 29, 1918, Ash Jr. was commissioned to 1st Lieutenant.

On August 28th Ash Jr. was transferred to the 24th Observation Squadron in Gondreville, France, 200 miles due East of Paris. The squadron was identified as an Army Observation Squadron, performing long-range, strategic reconnaissance over the entire length of the United States First Army Sector of the Western Front in France.

The groups first combat mission came on 12 September

1918 during the St. Mihiel Offensive, where Thomas engaged the enemy as a fighter pilot. Thirteen additional sorties were flown over the following ten days; a grueling experience.

The unit's first confirmed combat victory came on September 15, when 2d Lt. Roe E. Wells (Pilot) and 2d Lt. Albert W. Swinebroad (Observer) shot down a German aircraft. Over the eleven days of the offensive the unit lost only three aircraft, with two pilots captured.

Having proven himself, Ash Jr. was reassigned to the Vavincourt Aerodrome, France [Meuse-Argonne Sector] where he served in all major engagements until Armistice.

24th Aero Squadron, Vavincourt Aerodrome, France, Nov. 1918. Although not identified it is possible that Ash is in this photograph.

At Vavincourt Thomas was a member of the 139th Squadron, 2nd Pursuit Group, which had been organized on June 29th, 1918, just a few months prior to his arrival.

139th Aero Squadron, Belrain Aerodrome, France, November 1918. Thomas Ash is in the back row, third from left.

Staff of the 2nd Pursuit Group, Belrain Aerodrome, France, November 1918. Although not identified it is possible that Ash is in this photograph.

The group had become known for its' 132 air victories, 16 flying aces [credited with five or more kills], and 4 pilots decorated with the Distinguished Service Cross. While there Ash received official credit for downing an enemy Fokker aircraft at Marveuville, France on November 5, 1918, six days before the official end of hostilities.

The war effort over, the fighting group was officially demobilized in France on April 10, 1919. Four months prior to that event, Ash Jr. was aboard the ship North Carolina, departing from Best, France on January 18, 1919, with a destination port of Hoboken, New Jersey, the same port from which he had departed two years earlier.

With the world now at peace, the Panorama of Victory took place on May 3, 1919, in New York City. The parade of military personnel and equipment began at 110th Street [northern tip of Central Park] on Fifth Avenue and finished at Washington Square, a total length of five miles.

> *Every branch of the United States Army will take part. There will be eighty bands, including General Pershing's Headquarters Band and the Eleventh Cavalry's mounted band. The vast array of ordnance has been massed for two weeks at Van Cortland Park. Tanks, infantry, cavalry, motor lorries, moving machine shops, trench mortars, aeroplanes, and big guns will take part in the great "Panorama of Victory".* [153]

For the role he played in the celebratory gala, Thomas Ash was commended by the Director of the Air Service for directing a mimic battle between Army airplanes, a Fokker aircraft, and a dirigible. Ash Jr. was specifically cited for his 1500-foot parachute jump from the helium filled craft.

Since he had returned to the United States Lieutenant Ash had been actively engaged in supporting the Victory Loan campaigns which had been established after Armistice

---

[153] New York Times May 2, 1919. Panorama of Victory to be Five Miles Long. Page 5.

to help pay for the costly war. When the United States entered the war, the country had sold Liberty Bonds to fund the effort and had initiated an additional four Liberty Loan drives during the conflict.

The Victory Loan campaign was a post war effort to raise funds to offset the cost of the war effort.

On April 19, 1919, Thomas Ash Jr. and fifty other airmen from America, Britain, and France assembled in New York City at the headquarters of the American Flying Club at 11 East 38th Street.

The group had gathered to help send off seven of their brothers who would be performing aeronautics throughout northern New York State in support of the Victory Loan effort. The pilots would compete against each other in a race that would begin from Hazelhurst Field [Roosevelt Field on Long Island, New York – since closed] and travel, in sequence to Albany, Syracuse, Medina, Niagara Falls, Rochester, Utica, and finally conclude in Schenectady, New York.

While the group was gathered it was announced that, at 5:40 p.m., Eastern Standard Time, Captain Earl French White, Air Service, United States Army, had just completed the longest non-stop flight up to that time, flying from Ashburn Aviation Field, Chicago, Illinois to Hazelhurst Field, Mineola, Long Island, New York in 6 hours and 50 minutes. The crowd of assembled aviators erupted in cheers, and a seed was planted in the head of Thomas Ash Jr. as to the kind of emotions a success of this type could bring to airmen, and even to the country itself.

That seed would blossom later in life.

As best as can be determined Ash Jr. remained in the Army for a while working on the Victory campaign stock sales, as his occupation was recorded as "stock salesman" in the 1920 Federal Census while living in Manhattan. One of his fellow boarders, Dean Lamb, was identified as an "aviator" and may well have been associated with Thomas in some manner in recruitment efforts.

Ash's work might have taken him overseas as well as, on March 19, 1925, he was listed on the outbound S. S. President Roosevelt bound for Bremerhaven, a port on the northeastern coast of Germany. The ship manifest listed him as a "clerk", which certainly could have aligned nicely if he was traveling as a military representative. The purpose of the trip is unclear, and the date of the young man's return voyage remains elusive, although return he did.

By 1926, possibly earlier, Thomas Ash Jr. was assigned to and flying out of Selfridge Field, Harrison Township, Michigan for some purpose, possibly related to the military. Originally named Joy Aviation Field, the airfield was taken over by the Michigan National Guard on July 1, 1917, while World War I was raging in Europe.

After the war the Selfridge Air Base became a fighter plane training field, and home to the 94th Pursuit Squadron. Many other fliers such as the 1st Pursuit Group which had successful deployments during World War One found homes at Selfridge as well. In 1924, Charles Lindburg was assigned to the base to complete his reserve training.

World War I ace Capt. Eddie Rickenbacker, third from left, poses with other members of the 94th Pursuit Squadron, at Selfridge Field. (The Detroit News Archives)

By all accounts Thomas Ash was flying regular routes called Airways trips or Airways tours from Selfridge Air Base in the mid-1920s.

There are two possible definitions for these types of "named excursions", and each are referenced in the publication The Air Service Newsletter.[154]

The national newsletter was produced to:

> *...keep the personnel of the Air Service, both in Washington and in the field, informed as to the activities of the Air Service in general, and [was intended] for release to the public press.* [155]

---

[154] The Air Service Newsletter was the official newsletter of the U.S. Army Air Forces. It began publication in 1918 and reported on almost every aspect of army aviation during the "Golden Age of Flight".

[155] Air Service Newsletter, Volume 9, Number 1, Jan 7, 1925

The concept of an Airways tour permeates this publication with one possible definition being that it represented a planned air route to designated airports to ensure the viability of each as a safe and secure destination.

Identifying airports that met certain criteria would have potentially assisted in the development of establishing future air traffic hubs.

The second possibility is that Airways tours were associated with the Aeromarine Airways Corporation, as the company had begun to secure contracts from the United States Post Office Department to ferry mail between certain challenging locations. The company also had a vested interest in mining the potential of commercial transportation and had established passenger routes by the mid-1920s across the country.[156]

---

[156] Aeromarine Airways Corporation stock option pamphlet.

With either option a likely possibility, a report was filed in the Morning Herald of Uniontown, Pennsylvania in its February 3, 1926, edition:

Airmen Bring Message from Brother Flyer

Flying from Selfridge Field, Michigan, on a **regularly scheduled Airways trip,** *Lieutenants Victor S. Strahm, pilot, and Thomas Ash, Jr., landed at Burgess Field Sunday afternoon after hopping from Langin Field, Moundsville [West Virginia].*

Both officers brought messages from Lieutenant Collins of Selfridge Field, who was in attendance at the dedication of Burgess Field, extending his greetings to local friends.

One week later the same paper reported:

Birdmen Depart

Lieutenants Victor S. Strahm, pilot, and Thomas Ash, Jr., of Selfridge Field, Michigan, who have been detained at Burgess Field since last Sunday by bad weather, were able to hop off yesterday morning on their delayed flight to Mitchell Field, N. Y.

The officers were on a regularly scheduled Airways flight and were forced down here last Sunday afternoon owing to bad weather in the mountains near Somerfield. They expect to make the return flight over this city either Monday or Tuesday.

Chauncey Holt Co.

Lieutenant Thomas Ash at Selfridge Air Base (property of Holly Samociuk – used with permission)

Later that year, or possibly the next, Ash concluded his engagement in the military/National Guard and pursued a new adventure in Hollywood, California, as a stunt pilot in movie pictures, an occupation he continued for four years.

It was in Hollywood that he met talented, rich, and vivacious Ruth Wells Barron, a fellow pilot, who had been born in 1910.

The young woman had received her flight training in April of 1929, under Russell Holderman, at the Donald Woodward [D. W.] Flying Service which had opened earlier that same year in Leroy, New York. She was one of the first fifty students who had signed up for instruction.[157]

---

[157] Aviation Week. Woodward Course Opened. May 4, 1929.

Woodward Aviation Field, Leroy, New York, 1930. (Alan Reddig)

During World War I Holderman taught the art of flying to Army recruits at Hazelhurst [Roosevelt] Field on Long Island. After the end of the war, he worked for the United States Post Office Air Mail Service as both a mechanic and pilot.

In 1927 Holderman was asked by Donald Woodward, the son of the Jell-O magnate Orator Woodward, to design and build a private airport near Rochester, New York. He agreed and constructed the D.W. Airport at LeRoy, New York. Soon after the airport opened Holderman created the D.W. Flying Service and began to train pilots just as he had done earlier in his life.

Holderman was known as an extremely talented instructor, which was borne out by his personal instruction of Elinor Smith, who, after ten days of intense instruction achieved her solo piloting license at 16 years of age. She would go on to set, three months after her first solo flight, the official light plane altitude record of 11,889 feet. That same year, on a dare, she flew under all four of New York City's East River bridges.

It seemed that Holderman knew how to pick his pilots.

Six months after acquiring her piloting [transport] license, Ruth Barron, at the age of 20, entered the 1930 Women's National Air Derby which ran from Long Beach, California through the Southwest and Midwest to Chicago,

Illinois.

On the first leg of the race Barron came in at a close third place, besting far more experienced fliers.

Starters in the 1930 Women's National Air Derby from Long Beach, California to Chicago, Illinois. Left to Right: Marjorie Doig (Danbury, CT), Jean Le Rene (Chicago, IL), Ruth Stewart (St. Louis, MO), Ruth Barron (Hollywood, CA), Gladys O'Donnell (Long Beach, CA), Mildred Morgan (Beverly Hills, CA).

At the end of the second leg Barron had maintained her position.

The third leg was the demise of her pursuit for the

crown, as Barron overshot the target field due to a navigation error, landing 35 miles to the south at another airfield, arriving at the correct field the following day. Her mistake put her far behind the other competitors.

If not for her error, Barron would have likely placed fourth overall at the end of the race. But just finishing against the quality of the competition alone was an amazing accomplishment for such a young pilot.

Two years later, in 1931, Thomas Ash Jr., still toiling away as a stunt pilot on the West Coast, recalled the euphoria he, his fellow pilots, and the country had experienced when Captain White had completed his 1919 non-stop flight from Illinois to New York. The same emotions rushed back to him when he read of a transpacific flight contest run by the Asahi newspaper of Tokyo, Japan, with a winning prize of $25,000 ($460,000 in 2020).

Show me the money.

Ash was the first contestant to register.

The contest and Ash's registration took the country's imagination by storm. Newspapers in all fifty states reported on the upcoming event.

On April 17, 1931, Viscount Tadashiro Inouye introduced Thomas Ash as the **Pilot of the Pacific** as he spoke about the planned flight before the Pan-Pacific Club of Tokyo. Some of his words from his speech follow.

> *The purposes for which this club was founded, and my reason for coming to Japan are practically identical. Your earnest desire any my ardent wish is to be able to promote the lasting friendship between Japan and America.*

> *Up to the present time the Pacific Ocean, because of its immensity, has been a sort of barrier between two peoples living on its opposite borders. It is also the last great challenge to the aviation world. It is the peculiar province of aviation to break down the barrier of great distances, and at present it is my good fortune to be engaged in preparation not only to accept this challenge*

Viscount Tadashiro Inouye, first and continuous president of the Pan-Pacific Club of Tokyo for a decade. (Mid-Pacific magazine Dec 1930)

of a nonstop transpacific flight, but to do my small share in cementing the friendship existing between our two countries.

The preparations for this flight are very simple. You all probably know the plane, although it is now called the Pacific. With the assistance of my Japanese friends, we are putting it in the best possible condition. Mr. Nakura is lending me three of his mechanics. The Mitsubishi people are loaning me gasoline until my own arrives. The Asahi Shimbun [the most respected daily newspaper in Japan at that time] has assisted me in every possible manner. The army officers have volunteered their services. My friends in America are outdoing themselves on behalf of the flight. Nothing to my knowledge is being neglected, and on the day of the flight, both the plane and the motor will be as perfect as we can make them.

I want to thank you for your courtesy. Many of you have wished me well, for which I am sincerely grateful. I shall forget you. During the long watches of the night, when I am probably thousands of feet above the clouds and perhaps thousands of miles from shore, the memory of your good wishes will spur me to renewed courage. When I am cold and tired and very sleepy, and feeling very much alone, the thought of these villagers and fisherman and farmers at Sabushiro Beach [launching site] will inspire me to greater efforts, and I sincerely hope to bring this transpacific non-stop flight to a successful conclusion. [158]

At this point in the story, it is worthwhile to take a moment to consider the enormity of what had and what was about to occur.

A young man, with roots in the small town of Enfield, Connecticut, had addressed some of the most powerful men

---

[158] Mid-Pacific Magazine. April 17, 1931. Page 536.

in Japan at a revered organization as he accepted the challenge on behalf of all pilots to attempt a nonstop transpacific flight. This World War I American pilot had dared to attempt something that had never been done.

A kid from Enfield.

Let that sink in.

The April 23, 1931, edition of the Thompsonville Press reported on the anticipated event.

Local Flier to Try For Prize

Thomas Ash, Jr., a former resident of this town, registered this week with the newspaper Asahi of Tokio [sic Tokyo], Japan, as the first contestant in its prize of $25,000 for a non-stop flight from Japan to the United States. The venture is backed by Hon. John Buffelin of Tacoma, Wash. The proposed flight is from Tokio [sic Tokyo] to Seattle, Wash., a distance of 4,709 miles.

Mr. Ash served in the Army Air Corps during the World War, and was credited for bringing down three German planes.

For the past four years he has been "stunt" flying for the movies in Hollywood.

He is the son of Thomas Ash on Enfield Street. [159]

On May 26th newspapers on both sides of the country reported the arrival of Ruth Barron in Tokyo, Japan as she joined the entourage of individuals seeking to assist the aviator on his upcoming flight.[160]

---

[159] Thompsonville Press. April 23, 1931. Page 1.
[160] Stamford CT Daily Advocate (pg 1) & San Francisco Chronicle (Pg 3). May 26, 1931.

Each paper corrected earlier reports, made the previous week by vernacular newspapers [regional language newspapers], that Ms. Barron would be accompanying Ash Jr. on his transpacific flight, perhaps as a co-pilot. Barron had later changed her statement to clarify that she was there in a support role only, and the Daily Advocate reported:

She had known Ash in Hollywood and had come to Japan to assist him in any way possible. [161]

But was that really the case?

There is no record of any romantic relationship between Barron and Ash, although the former lived on Finley Avenue and the latter on Hillhurst Avenue just a few blocks away from each other, so distance certainly wasn't an impediment.

In addition to her piloting skills, it was reported that Barron was an actress, although there is no record of her being in a movie even though she lived in Hollywood. It is possible Ash had gotten her stunt piloting roles in movies, as he made his living in that manner and certainly had the contacts, so certainly the relationship could certainly have been one based on mutual respect.

Years later, in the Rochester Democrat and Chronicle July 4, 1936, edition, added fuel to the speculation that might have been Barron's true intentions:

In 1931 she left her commercial flying and racing in Hollywood and with Capt. [sic Lieutenant] Ash went to Tokyo, determined to be the first woman to fly the Pacific. [162]

Later in that same article:

---

[161] Stamford CT Daily Advocate May 26, 1931. Page 1.
[162] Rochester Democrat and Chronicle July 4, 1936.

Never did Mrs. Nason [Ruth Barron] quite abandon her dream of a transpacific flight.

Less than a year ago [1935], several Municipal Airport flyers helped her in an effort to find a suitable plane. At that time she was happy but uncommunicative, merely letting it be generally understood that she had found a backer.

Later she announced that it was "all off". She dreamed of a Japan to San Francisco flight, non-stop.
163

In retrospect, the more likely scenario was that Barron, having known that Ash had entered the transpacific flight contest, took it upon herself to travel to Japan to see if she could somehow convince Ash to let her accompany him on the Pacific adventure. Her actions were most likely based on her relationship with the flyer and on the belief that he would accommodate her dream.

Barron had been rebuffed the previous year by the National Aeronautical Association in her attempt to break the gender barrier at the Buffalo [New York] Air Races in September of 1935.

The transpacific venture could have represented an opportunity for her to establish her credentials as a female pilot in a foreign country where the NAA held no sway. After all, she had been granted a license to fly in Japan by that government, the only woman to have that luxury, even though an Army escort was required when she flew.

But Ash had rebuffed her as well, and she recanted her earlier statement to the foreign press, thus giving up her dream at that time.

All was not lost to the aviatrix, though, as she met the

---

163 Rochester Democrat and Chronicle July 4, 1936.

American Vice Consul William Franklin Nason while there and married him in January of the following year.

On May 28th, the San Francisco Chronicle, San Diego Union, San Diego Evening Tribune, Thompsonville Press, Hartford Courant, and San Jose Evening News all carried articles about the upcoming flight. Each paper reported that Ash would leave Tachikawa Airdrome the following day and land at Samushiro beach, from where the transpacific flight would begin.

The plane, acquired by Ash from the previous pilot who had failed in his attempt to cross the Pacific, proved more cumbersome than newer models.

To address one of the shortcomings the plane was outfitted with an experimental two-wheeled dolly which would reduce tail drag and hopefully allow the plane to reach the ground speed necessary for takeoff. The fuel required for the jump, 1020 gallons, added a great deal of weight to the craft and represented another challenging consideration.

On May 29th, the San Diego Evening Tribune, the Imperial Valley Press, the Riverside Daily Press, the Stamford Daily Advocate, the San Diego Union, and the San Francisco Chronicle, among others across the country, reported on the day's activities. Ruth Barron, possibly because of the presumed slight and badly bruised ego, chose not to accompany Ash on his hop to Samushiro beach, opting instead on returning to California by steamer the following week.

The Imperial Valley Press noted that the plane had essentially been gutted to reduce weight, which offered another possibility as to why Barron had been excluded from the flight.

The runway at Samushiro beach had been built to a

length of one mile to accommodate the weight of the plane and the predicted difficulty of takeoff.

The start of the 4,400-mile non-stop flight was set for 7 AM the following morning, Friday, May 30, 1931. At the appointed time, Ash postponed his takeoff due to unfavorable crosswinds, and set a new start time for the following day between 4 and 6 AM when the local fisherman agreed that the air would be most calm.[164]

And then, on June 1, 1931, Thomas Ash Jr. called off the attempt, abandoning the proposed non-stop flight, the plane, as configured, was unable to rise from the makeshift beach runway.

Ash's call followed the decision to reduce the plane's fuel to 900 gallons as the engine had failed to meet the 1850 revolutions necessary to achieve liftoff with the original fuel load. The reduction in fuel also meant a recalculation and adjustment for a new target destination of Dutch Harbor, Alaska rather than Seattle, Washington.

But finally, even with all of the last-minute modifications, it was deemed mathematically impossible for the Pacific to even reach Puget Sound with the reduced fuel load and lower prop rotation, never mind Alaska itself.

Ash was despondent and decided to return to Tokyo.

Two unlikely men entered the breech – Cecil Allen, 27, a former washing machine salesman who taught himself air navigation, and Don Moyle, 29, a motorcycle repairman who learned to pilot airplanes while he worked as a mechanic at the Santa Ana, California airfield.

As Thomas Ash Jr. pulled out of the contest, these two

---

[164] San Diego Evening Tribune. May 30, 1931. Page 5.

men stepped in, with backing from multiple people, one of which was the brother of Moyle's fiancée, Miss Francis Bresson of Riverside, California. They acquired Ash's plane and spent a few weeks rebuilding the craft, addressing the structural and mechanical issues they believed most pressing.

To address the lack of power which had ultimately doomed Ash's liftoff attempt, they added a supercharger to the existing engine which increased the horsepower from 425 to 525.[165] Lift had been increased by removing an inch from the end of each propeller and by installing a new tail group.[166]

Should the duo fail in their attempt, two more airmen, Hugh Herndon and Clyde Pangborn, waited in the wings, having requested and awaited permission to attempt their own transpacific flight.

With little fanfare Allen and Moyle successfully took off from the same airstrip that had been prepared for the Thomas Ash Jr. at 4:30 AM on September 7, 1931, Tokyo time. Their liftoff time and flight plan had been the same as had been projected and previously filed by the Enfield Ace.

The craft carried the same fuel total as had Ash, 1020 gallons, which the duo had estimated would provide 47 hours of flying time based on a consumption rate of 22 gallons per hour, even with the additional weight of a copilot.

An hour and a half after takeoff the craft was seen above Point Erimo, Hokkaido Island, 110 miles north of Samushiro Beach, right in line with their target speed of 100

---

[165] San Diego Union. Cutters Hunt Missing Fliers Overdue on Japan-U.S. Hop. September 10, 1931. Page 3.
[166] Denver Post. Tokio-Seattle Flight Started by Americans. September 8, 1931. Page 6.

miles per hour.

At Boeing Field in Seattle, Washington, 55 hours later, there was no sign of the airplane, and the duo were more than eight hours overdue. The aviation enthusiasts gathered at the field were more than uncomfortable at that point and expected to hear the worst.

The Coast Guard sent out more than eight vessels into the Pacific to begin search and rescue operations.

> *"It is an almost impossible task," said Captain [H. D.] Hinckley, "but the Coast Guard is used to them and we are glad to undertake it. We'll do the best we can — but I am afraid it will not be enough."* [167]

Bressen's brother though, remained hopeful:

> *"My guess is just as good as anyone else's," he asserted with very much the air of a small boy whistling in the dark, "and I've got a hunch that they ran short of gas and landed somewhere in the Aleutians."* [168]

Others, especially seasoned pilots, were far less hopeful. Ash himself considered that the supercharger that had been added to the engine might have added too much strain and might have caused the engine to fail at some point.

And then, nine days after they had been given up as lost; a message was transmitted from the Russian steamer Beriat and received at the United States Naval Radio Station on St. Paul Island in the Bering Sea.

The transmission, also received by the Coast Guard

---

[167] San Diego Union. Cutters Hunt Missing Fliers Overdue on Japan-U.S. Hop. September 10, 1931. Page 3.
[168] IBID

Cutter while on patrol in the Bering Sea searching for the fliers, said that the pair and their plane had landed safely on Navarin Island.

NEW HOPE FOR HAPPY ENDING

Cecil A Allen

Don Moyle

Miss Frances Bresson

The actual story was a bit more convoluted.

Shortly after their sighting over Point Erimo, the weather turned for the worse. A gale had exploded over the Aleutian Islands, and the duo fought for 20 hours to keep the plane aloft, finally landing the craft on an island where they waited out the storm for seven days.

On the eighth day they took off and flew due north, landing near the fishing village of Miano Pilgino, Siberia, southwest of Cape Navarin, and latitudinally opposite Nome, Alaska. Cape Navarin was 500 miles off course from the original flight plan.

After a refueling from a Russian steamer, Moyle and Allen resumed their ill-fated flight on September 18, 1931, to Nome, Alaska. From there the pair would head to Tacoma, Washington to reconnect with the major backer of the excursion John Buffelen, a Tacoma businessman.

A particular transmission though, to Frances Bresson, fiancée of Moyle, bothered reporters and would spur later speculation of a grand hoax.

> *"Landed on uninhabited island. Everything alright. Have Frank put publicity man on the job. Will be in Seattle September 22."* [169]

The public perception of the pair had begun to sour, as the Seattle Daily Times, in an Editorial embedded in the lead story *Battle in Wild Gale Above Sea Described*, noted:

EDITORIAL

> *"Get the publicity man on the job"* was the first message that Moyle and Allen sent back to

---

[169] Omaha World Herald. Pacific Fliers Found Safe After a Week. September 17, 1931. Page 4.

civilization after being "lost" on the shores of the Pacific Ocean.

The publicity man's job apparently will be to convince the public that there is something heroic about flying around the north rim of the Pacific Ocean in three or four hops. [170]

Adding insult to injury, the Seattle Daily Times took another swipe at the pair a few weeks later, after they experienced another unforced error.

Tacoma's Fete for Moyle and Allen Slips Up

Reception Planned for Two Flyers Turns to 'Comedy of Errors' as They Come Too Soon to Wrong Field

Those Bad Luck Boys – *Don Moyle and Cecil Allen* – *arrived by plane from Tokyo twenty-nine days late and two hours early. And thereby hangs a pathetic tale.*

The two fliers were supposed to land at the Pierce County Airport in Tacoma, Washington at approximately 6:30 PM to a great reception. Instead, the duo had mistakenly landed at the Mueller-Harkins Airport in Tacoma, Washington at 4:20 PM, four miles from the intended destination. There they were found by a reporter, the two pilots sitting alone, dejected, on a bench.

Eventually Buffelen, the financial backer, arrived by car, climbed aboard the plane with his arial proteges, and guided them as they returned to the air, landing within a few minutes at the correct airfield.

Perhaps Buffelen should have taken off with the pair on

---

[170] Seattle Daily Times. Battle in Wild Gale Above Sea Described. September 18, 1931. Page 1.

the first leg of the trip from Japan.

The inexperienced Moyle and Allen had turned the once noble pursuit into a comedic affair.

One can only wonder what might have been had Thomas Ash successfully lifted off from Samushiro beach months earlier.

One year later, on June 16, 1932, newspapers across the country reported on the possibility of an exciting new adventure.

> **_Thomas Ash Jr. had applied to the State Department for permission to fly over foreign territory, his eyes on the Post-Gatty globe_** _circling record of eight days, 15 hours, and 51 minutes._ [171]

Perhaps the last chapter had yet to be written.

---

[171] The Atlanta Journal. June 16, 1932. Page 22.
The Nome Nugget. May 14, 1932. Page 7.
The Evening Star [Washington DC]. June 16, 1932. Page 1.

11: CLICK BAIT

Oh! the old swimmin'-hole! whare the crick so still and deep

Looked like a baby-river that was laying half asleep,

And the gurgle of the worter round the drift jest below

Sounded like the laugh of something we onc't ust to know

Before we could remember anything but the eyes

Of the angels lookin' out as we left Paradise;

But the merry days of youth is beyond our controle,

And it's hard to part ferever with the old swimmin'-hole.[172]

The swimming hole conjures up pictures of laughing naked boys leaping from a hardpacked creek bed into the cool waters of a stream as it pauses, gathered in a deep pool on its inevitable journey to the ocean.

The images we recall are rooted in the late 1800s and

---

[172] James Whitcomb Riley (pen name Benjamin F. Johnson of Boone County) *The Old Swimmin' Hole. 1883.*

early 1900s, before towns and villages began to manage the activities of children and remove the sense of risk and adventure from social sports.

The "Ole Swimming Hole" Way To Be Cool

The 'Ole Swimmin' Hole of fact, fiction, and fancy is cool, cool reality to Dan Klezos, Bruce Lynch and company as they dive into the Scantic near the Town Farm Road. With the thermometer climbing into the 90's and the long Fourth of July weekend ahead, a goodly percentage of the Town's residents are "sweating it out" until they get to their favorite swimming holes in some lake, stream or along the beach.

Thompsonville Press July 2, 1958, recalls joy of swimming holes.

Swimming holes are a different experience than beaches or riverbanks. They are secluded spots, closely guarded and magical, known only to, and experienced by, "locals" or other kids lucky enough to be invited to join in on a hot summer day.

The pools are cold and dark, fed by upstream waters sourced from ponds, lakes, or tributaries which are replenished by rains or underground aquifers on cycles determined by the whims of nature.

Thompsonville had its secret waters, carved out along the winding Freshwater Brook, hidden from the prying eyes of the outside world. Swimming holes known only to the same youths who roamed the narrow streets named Pleasant, High, School, and Main; or North Main which ran east, out of town.

The pools were named for those whose land abutted them, like Phil Downey's [Doughney[173]] Swimming Hole[174], or for some attribute like Twenty Foot[175] or Deep Hole[176].

Their location was carefully guarded, and even today we can only recover small bits of information that might lead us to the correct spot.

Well known to many, yet unknown to most.

In summertime the spot having the greatest attraction was a pool in the fresh water brook called (I never knew why) "twenty foot". It was only a jolly run along the road, then down the meadow, and we were on grassy banks. Here was depth for boys of any age; a place where the fellow had to lie down in order to get wet, and a few feet away was that dreadful, but fascinating, spot where it was "over your head".

What runs we had along the banks of that pretty brook as free from clothes as when we came into this world. What horrors faced us when the big boys pulled us out into deep water! How bold we felt ourselves when we waded out to where the water reached our

---

[173] Misspelling – Philip Doughney of Irish descent was a tobacco farmer in Enfield then Suffield. Wife Mary. Ancestry.com

[174] Thompsonville Press *Old Time Resident Writes From Coast* March 2, 1922. Page 2.

[175] Thompsonville Press Feb 20, 1896. Page 2. Thompsonville Press Sept. 24, 1908. Page 2.

[176] Thompsonville Press June 14, 1923. Page 3

chin; and who will ever forget his first dive from the bank? [177]

The article provides a couple of clues as to the swimming hole's location. It was only a jolly run east from, one assumes, the center of town, and:

Ten minutes' walk farther out there were Kingsberry's woods. [178]

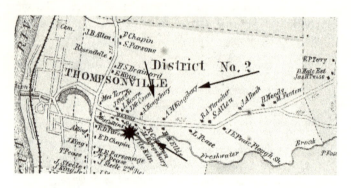

Possible location of Twenty Foot swimming hole (based on Thompsonville Press articles).

Another article provides a few more clues.

The way to "Twenty Foot" is known to every boy hereabouts. It would be hard to tell when that goal of a summer afternoon was named, or which were the earliest generations that beat out a path that wends along the edge of the brook. When one leaves the highway by the bridge and turns into the field no sign forbidding trespassing bars the way, a fact that arouses no one's gratitude to the owner of the property, who seems thus to yield that immemorial privilege of

---

[177] Thompsonville Press Feb 20, 1896. Page 2.
[178] IBID

crossing private estates, gained the world over by the persistent habit of generations. [179]

A post in a later newspaper article seems to confirm the location as noted in the previous map.

That "stop" sign down at the intersection of Enfield and High Streets [has] been pointing in the wrong direction. As it now stands it would only indicate a "stop" direction for a rowboat coming down Freshwater Brook from the old swimming hole of years ago. [180]

The location of the *Deep Hole* swimming hole is more of a mystery, but it is assuredly separate from *Twenty-Foot* based on another article.

How times have changed! Who can forget "Deep Hole", one of the greatest swimming places that one could have. And who could forget "20-foot" and the other recesses of Freshwater Brook way back yonder in the lots where one could enjoy the balm of a sunny afternoon with complete comfort and gusto. [181]

The article seems to suggest that Deep Hole might somehow be apart from Freshwater Brook, but, of course, provides no further details as to its location.

An earlier Thompsonville Press article though, does add information that might lead to a generalized location.

Youngsters to Lose Old Freshwater Swimming Hole

"Deep Hole" in Freshwater Brook, for many years a

---

[179] Thompsonville Press Sept. 24, 1908. Page 2.

[180] Thompsonville Press May 26, 1938. Page 2.

[181] Thompsonville Press June 14, 1933. Page 3.

favorite swimming hole for the younger boys of the town, can no longer be used for that purpose.

The public dump, recently established by the town on the J. F. O'Hear property in Enfield Street, drains directly into the brook near the swimming hole and has contaminated the water so that it is unsafe for swimming.

This was brought to the attention of the authorities last week when several boys who had been swimming there suffered a severe rash.

The health authorities will likely post the place against swimming as a precaution for the boy's health and safety. [182]

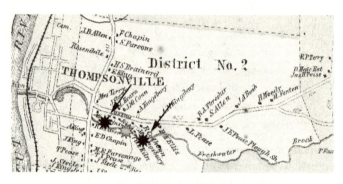

The Deep Hole swimming hole was located in one of two possible locations – either before or after the Twenty Foot (in grey) hole. O'Hear had or built on properties in both locations, although there are records of a public dump on the star closer to the pond.

Before the "new dump" on the O'Hear property was established there was a public dumping ground, privately owned but publicly managed, at the corner of Alden Avenue

---

[182] Thompsonville Press June 14, 1923. Page 8.

and Enfield Street[183].

> *A notice has been served on John A. Best, owner of the public dumping ground on Alden Avenue and Enfield Street, to remove all inflammable materials from the dump within 20 days.* [184]

Even the First Selectman contributed refuse.

> *On last Saturday afternoon while dumping rubbish at the public dump at the corner of Alden Avenue and Springfield Road [Enfield Street], a pair of First Selectman Albert J. Epstein's horses were dragged back over the 35-foot embankment.* [185]

Dumps were subject to minimal "regulations" or standards of practice, more reflective of health concerns than environmental impact.

> *As a matter of routine duty, it is the practice of the heath Officer to make a careful inspection of the public dump each week.*
>
> *It is far easier to prevent complaints than to stop them after they are made. It is only by the exercise of great care and constant watchfulness that we have been able to maintain our dump in its present location for so long a time. Just as soon as conditions warrant is a strenuous protest against this location will be made and we shall find ourselves seeking a new site. We can hardly find one so convenient.* [186]

---

[183] Thompsonville Press April 19, 1922. Page 4.

[184] Thompsonville Press August 24, 1922. Page 5.

[185] Thompsonville Press January 4, 1917. Page 1.

[186] Thompsonville Press May 7, 1914. Page 1.

Attention

Storekeepers and Housekeepers of Thompsonville

Owing to the rules of the state and local boards of health, the burning of paper and paper boxes of any kind besides wet garbage, will not be burned at the public dumping ground in the future.

For this reason the garbage collectors will not take any more of this so-called refuse on collection days.

Also all trimmings of trees will be refused by the collectors.

Kindly govern yourselves accordingly and oblige.

Signed,

JAMES T. MURRAY,
GEORGE H. PAYNE,
LOUIS HAWTHORNE,
Selectmen Town of Enfield.

Dated at Enfield, Ct., April 7, 1923.

It seems as if the 1914 article predicted the location change of the public dump in 1924 but perhaps not the consequences of the garbage effluent to the Deep Hole recreational swimmers.

Beyond the leaching of garbage into the brook there were other health concerns of the time, as an article in the September 25, 1924, issue of the Thompsonville Press recalled.

"At times during the past year our town seemed to be a veritable storm center for contagious diseases; mild epidemics of Measles, Scarlet Fever, Whooping Cough, Chicken Pox being in full swing at the same time.

Owing to the temporary pollution of the Freshwater Pond, which it is estimated will take a couple of seasons to correct, no ice was cut from this pond which has been a source of supply for many years."

Of concern as well was the development and transmission of Smallpox throughout the state, although vaccinations were underway. Thankfully Polio wouldn't be a worry for another 25 years.

The article concluded with a general health directive:

Care should be exercised to keep the moist and the dry garbage carefully separated as we want nothing of an offensive nature carried to the public dump.

Beyond infective fluids from public dumps compromising the purity of Freshwater Brook, the reckless activities of Thompsonville youths were gaining the attention of the community thereby jeopardizing the unregulated use of the brook, the swimming holes, and even the Connecticut River as well.

> *Means for avoiding, if possible, a repetition of the drowning accidents which have occurred more or less frequently at the Enfield Falls, where two boys lost their lives Sunday, were discussed by the governing board, and it was voted to request the selectman to have life boards and ropes placed near the falls, where they could be readily accessible in case of emergency. It was also voted to ask the selectmen to have similar precautions taken at the* **various swimming holes** *along the riverbank.* [187]

Due to overwhelming townwide concerns, by 1925 the town had decided a proposed public swimming pool was a safer option for all concerned.

The swimming holes would be relegated to memory.

It certainly had nothing to do with the reported 1916 shark attack on Freshwater Brook.

Or did it?

It's a common belief that sharks don't frequent fresh water, and for most of the species that is true. A delicate balance of salt to water must be maintained in their bodies, or they bloat and die.

But not the bull shark.

Bull sharks, almost exclusively, have evolved in such a way that their kidneys are able to recycle the salt within their bodies which enables them to live in fresh water.

---

[187] Thompsonville Press July 17, 1924. Page 1.

Not forever. But long enough to hunt and feed.

Matawan is a small town 11 miles inland from the eastern coast of New Jersey. It is connected to the Atlantic Ocean by way of a winding, narrow tidal waterway called the Matawan Creek, a tributary not unlike Freshwater Brook in depth and profile.

On the early afternoon of July 12, 1916, 11-year-old Lester Stillwell met some friends for a swim at Matawan Creek. The summer heat had driven boys to the refreshing waters of the swimming hole as it had thousands of other youths all over the country.

A way to cool off "au natural".

When the dozen or so boys in the creek saw Lester raise his hands above the water and scream, they thought he was just kidding around, drawing attention to himself as boys of that age are wont to do.

That was until the water turned red all around him.

And his screaming didn't stop.

Stanley Fisher, a 300 pound 24-year-old leapt from the riverbank into the water, unaware of the terror that would greet him as he made his way toward the struggling youth.

In mere moments Fisher's lower leg was torn from his body and he began to sink below the surface, the water swirling around him.

A third youth leapt into the creek and pulled Fisher to the safety of the shore.

The would-be savior, Stanley Fisher, bled out and died within moments on the shoreline.

Lester Stillwell's body was found two days later, at low

tide, 150 yards upstream.

The upper half of his body anyway.

The lower half had been consumed.

Residents of Matawan search the river for the missing Stillwell.

Downstream, not half a mile away from where Stillwell and Fisher had been attacked, Joseph Ralph Dunn, who was visiting his aunt at Cliffside, leapt from the pier of the New Jersey Brick Company into the brackish waters of Matawan Creek.

Alongside him was a boy of about the same age, Jerry Harrihan, who, like Dunn, had sought relief from the stifling heat in the cool waters.

A call erupted from a passing motorboat for the boys to leave the stream. Harrihan, closer to shore, responded quickly.

Dunn attempted to comply but was yanked backwards,

pulled momentarily under. Harrihan reentered the water and, grabbing Dunn's arm, pulled the boy to shore, the flesh stripped from his lower leg.

He would somehow survive.

The sanctity of the swimming hole had been broken by a ravenous monster from the deep.

It wasn't just the shorelines that were unsafe that summer of 1916, but the creeks, tributaries, and swimming playgrounds of America's youth.

In Elizabeth, New Jersey, a bull shark was shot and killed while it maneuvered in the Elizabeth River, close to Staten Island, New York. It was the only shark ever to be captured in the freshwater stream.

On July 13th a five-foot shark was captured in a small inlet near Fairfield Beach in Connecticut, not far from one of the most popular recreational swimming areas. It was the second shark caught within seven days.[188]

At Indian Neck in Branford, Connecticut, wary bathers scoured the waters of the shore resort Montowese House for signs of predators.[189] Likewise beachgoers at nearby Pine Orchard kept a sharp eye for signs of activity on Long Island Sound.

Bathers at Watch Hill, Rhode Island remained cautious.

At the Griswold Inn in Essex, Connecticut, workers moved forward to install a wire mesh shark barricade to secure the beach from possible shark attacks.[190]

Reports are frequent of sharks being seen off resorts, and

---

[188] Hartford Courant. July 14, 1916. Page 1.

[189] Hartford Courant. July 23, 1916. Page 18.

[190] IBID

one five feet in length is reported to have been killed off the Thimble Islands [Branford, Connecticut], ten miles east of here.[191]

In Stamford, Connecticut, a shark partly ate its way through netting installed to protect the bathing beach of millionaire John Sherman Hoyt before the beast became enmeshed and died.[192]

The less wealthy couldn't afford the protection of steel mesh nettings available to those who lived on the shoreline or frequented seaside resorts.

Certainly not children of mill towns like Thompsonville whose swimming holes were potential feeding grounds.

And just like that, as if someone had predicted it; there, on the front page of the August 3, 1916, edition of the Thompsonville Press.

May Have Been Shark blazoned above the fold on the weekly newspaper. **Brook Being Patrolled**.

Enfield has been suspected for some years as cherishing a certain conceit as a summer resort.

---

[191] New Britain Herald July 14, 1916. Page 1.
[192] Springfield Daily News. August 17, 1916. Page 12.

But all of this has passed.

Enfield has come to the front, we have arrived.

We have a shark. [193]

The article went on to discuss that two young boys, residents of West Street, had recently decided to learn how to swim.

Knowing full well that every embryo citizen of Enfield residing in District 1, had, for unknown generations acquired this [skill] in [the] "Twenty-foot" swimming hole, they repaired hitherto.

Soon little piles of discarded boyish garments decorated the muddy bank of the pool, and two little naked bodies were stirring up the muck in this murky old swimming hole.

Things [grew] pleasantly interesting when there was a decided commotion in the water at the lower end of the pool.

There is no record of anyone having gotten out of that swimming hole in less time than it took those two boys.

They didn't seem to care much about their clothes as they made a break across lots to some men who were hoeing tobacco nearby.

...between gasps of breath...the boys [revealed they] had seen a greenish black fish about fifteen feet long, [with] teeth from one to six inches long.

The men had no difficulty in deciding that Freshwater Brook, more, that "Twenty-foot," hallowed in the memory of generations of anxious

---

[193] Thompsonville Press August 3, 1916. Page 1.

mothers and fathers as the symbol of safety and security, had been invaded by a man-eating shark.

All hands rushed to the pool. [194]

The group arrived, and scanned the waters, but saw no obvious sign of the predator.

Thomas W. Moore, a local ornithologist, is patrolling the brook every hour of low tide. Tom says it is rather unusual for a shark to go up Freshwater Brook, especially during such warm weather…Although he [says] that he has seen sharks do some strange things out west in the irrigating ditches.

He figures the shark is …in the dark water back of the Heine's old bottling place, in which case he is sure to get him. If he has swum up to the wilds of Jabbok of course the chances of a capture are remote.

The incident has, as a matter of course, caused much excitement and no little fear in the community.

…we are hugging to our heart the one precious thought that as a health resort Enfield has at least has a startling sensation, a sensation so thrilling, so shivery, so exquisitely unusual and unexpected, so out of the ordinary, that it is sure to be a drawing card. [195]

And that was the end of it.

No more reported sightings at any swimming holes or anywhere along the Freshwater Brook, despite the newspaper report or exhortations of the local authorities.

---

[194] Thompsonville Press August 3, 1916. Page 1.
[195] Thompsonville Press August 3, 1916. Page 1.

There were no follow up letters to the editor expressing concern for the safety of the children or questions about sensible precautions families should consider.

But then there were obvious questions for the less gullible when considering the story as reported.

There was not, to anyone's knowledge, a *Heine's old bottling place* anywhere in town, and no one could recall ever meeting anyone named Thomas W. Moore.

The two youths mentioned in the story, *Paulus Jamfrisky* and *Stanislaw Groundglassky*, were not listed as students in any Enfield school.

And then there was the question of how a fifteen-foot bull shark might have made its way up the Connecticut River and into the Freshwater Brook.

Was the article real? Fancy?

Had a veritable *P. T. Barnum* been visited upon the Thompsonville Press readers?

Those were questions for other days and were not worrisome concerns for boys who still felt the need to shed their clothes and dive into the cool waters of a swimming hole under the sweltering summer sun.

Perhaps, though, with at least one eye scanning the waters for an upright fin…

INDEX

REFERENCES

Amit R. Paley, "The Secret Court of 1920, Part I" & "The Secret Court of 1920, Part II" November 21, 2002, accessed March 2, 2023

Biennial Report of the Attorney-General. (1919). United States: State of Connecticut.

Boyle, Sheila Tully; Bunie, Andrew (October 1, 2005). Paul Robeson: The Years of Promise and Achievement. University of Massachusetts Press.

Braude, Ann. News From the Spirit World: A Checklist of American Spiritualist Periodicals, 1847-1900. American Antiquarian Society Proceedings. Volume 99. Issue 2 (January 1, 1990)

Cammarata, Christine. M. (Ed.). (2020, October). Suicide (for teens) - nemours kidshealth. KidsHealth. Retrieved March 11, 2023, from https://kidshealth.org/en/teens/suicide.html.

Carvalho, Joseph III (2022) Italians in WesternMassachusetts: The FirstGenerations: 1814 - 1941. Academia Edu. Retrieved April 3, 2023 from https://www.academia.edu/26492314/Italians_in_Wes tern_Massachusetts_The_First_Generations_docx

Catalogue. (1905). Wesleyan University (Middletown, Conn.) · 1905. United States: (n.p.).

Chemical & Metallurgical Engineering Volume 32, November 1925. McGraw Hill Co., Inc. (publisher). H. C. Parmalee editor.

Clark, B. (2006). Enfield, Connecticut: Stories Carved in Stone. United States: Dog Pond Press.

Davis, F. C., Davis, R. W. (1973). Somers: The History of a Connecticut Town. United States: Somers Historical Society.

Duberman, Martin B. (1989). Paul Robeson. Bodley Head.

Ellis, Lee and Walsh, Anthony (2003). *Crime, Delinquency and Intelligence: A Review of Worldwide Literature.* The Scientific Study of General Intelligence: Tribute to Arthur R. Jensen pp 343-365.

Enfield's Shaker Legacy - Connecticut history: A CT Humanities project. (2022, August 15). Retrieved March 21, 2023, from https://connecticuthistory.org/enfields-shaker-legacy/

Fraser, James W., Pedagogue for God's Kingdom: Lyman Beecher and the Second Great Awakening (New York: University Press of America, 1985), 17, 19.

From ice harvesting to Icebox. (2022, February 17). Retrieved March 26, 2023, from https://www.jaxhistory.org/from-ice-harvesting-to-icebox/

Gibbs, Charles S., Massachusetts Agricultural Experiment Station. Poultry Science, VOL. XIII, No. 4. Sexing Baby Chicks. July 1934. Page 208.

Gibbs, C. S. A Guide to Sexing Chicks. Orange Judd Publishing Company Inc., New York (1935).

Grant, E. S. (1984). The Club on Prospect Street: A History of the Hartford Club. United States: Hartford Club.

Hall, William H. *The History of West Hartford.* Published by The West Hartford Chamber of Commerce. Hartford, Connecticut. 1930.

Hawes-Cooper Act. St. James Encyclopedia of Labor History Worldwide: Major Events in Labor History and Their Impact. Retrieved January 16, 2023 from

Encyclopedia.com:
https://www.encyclopedia.com/history/encyclopedias
-almanacs-transcripts-and-maps/hawes-cooper-act

Ile de la tortue, Histoire. Petite histoire de l'île de la tortue. Villa Camp Mandingue. Haiti. Retrieved 01 March 2023. http://www.campmandingue.com/ile%20de%20la%20 tortue-histoire.htm

Inter-Maritime Forwarding Co. v. United States, 1957, U.S. Customs Court, C.D. 1897, 39 Cust. Ct. 17, July 16, 1957

Letters, J. and. (2013, September 12). "beautiful and important wonders": The shakers and spiritualism. Shaker Heritage Society. Retrieved March 19, 2023, from https://home.shakerheritage.org/beautiful-important-wonders-shakers-spiritualism/

Massachusetts Agricultural Experiment Station, Amherst. Annual Report, Bulletin No. 305, March 1934 (Fiscal Year Ending November 30, 1933)

Melton, J. Gordon, ed. (2001). Encyclopedia of Occultism & Parapsychology. Vol. 2 (5th ed.). US: Gale Group. p. 1463.

Mission & History | Hopkins School. (n.d.). Www.hopkins.edu. Retrieved January 18, 2023, from https://www.hopkins.edu/about-us/mission--history

New England Spiritualist: A Journal of the Methods and Philosophy of Spirit-manifestation, and its uses to mankind. 1855-1857 Weekly. Boston, MA. Editor: Alonzo E. Newton, (editor and publisher).

Prison Farm System Hit and Defended. (1947, July 16). *The Hartford Courant.* P 1.

Public Documents of the State of Connecticut. (1905). United States: order of the General Assembly.

Report of the State Board of Charities: Public Documents of the State of Connecticut. Volume 3. Part 2. 1905

Redmond, George F. (1922). Financial Giants of America (Volume 1). The Stratford Company (publisher)

Robeson, Paul Jr. (July 9, 2001). The Undiscovered Paul Robeson, An Artist's Journey, 1898–1939. John Wiley & Sons

Scientific American. (1868). United States: Munn & Company. Volume 18.

Stortz, Martha Ellen (1996). "Ritual Power, Ritual Authority: Configurations and Reconfigurations in the Era of Manifestations". In Aune, Michael Bjerknes; DeMarinis, Valerie M. (eds.). Religious and Social Ritual: Interdisciplinary Explorations. SUNY Press. pp. 105–135.

Szymanski, A.-M. (2005). Stop, Thief! Private Protective Societies in Nineteenth-Century New England. The New England Quarterly, 78(3), 407–439. http://www.jstor.org/stable/30045548

The Budget Report of the State Board of Finance and Control to the General Assembly, Session of [1929-] 1937. (1919). United States.

The Shaker Manifesto. (1882). United States: United Societies.

The Spiritual Telegraph (1855). (Volume Seven). *Cures By Spirits*. Partridge & Britain Publishers, 300 Broadway, N.Y. N.Y.. S. B. Britain editor.

The Two Worlds: A Journal Devoted to Spiritualism, Occult Science, Ethics, Religion and Reform. Published by William Britten: The Lindens, Manchester.

Thompson, J. S. (1904). History of Composing Machines: A Complete Record of the Art of Composing Type by

Machinery...also Lists of Patents on Composing Machines, American and British, Chronologically Arranged. United Kingdom: Inland Printer Company.

TreasureNet.com accessed March 1, 2023. https://www.treasurenet.com/threads/the-neptune.41624/#post-6540792

United States Department of the Interior National Park, Service National Register of Historic Places, Somersville Historic District, Tolland County, Connecticut. Section 8. Page 3.

Weisberg, Barbara. (2004). Talking to the Dead : Kate and Maggie Fox and the Rise of Spiritualism (1st ed.). Harper. SanFrancisco

Welsh, C. (1918). Draper's Self Culture: Morals, manners, business and civics. United States: Twentieth century self culture association.

Whipping and Castration as punishments for Crime (June 1899) Yale Law Journal (vol VIII no 9)

Local Newspaper Archives:

- The Thompsonville Press
- The Springfield Republican
- The Springfield Daily News
- The Springfield Union
- The Hartford Courant

ABOUT THE AUTHOR

Peter Floyd Sorenson was born in Sleepy Hollow, New York in 1957.

He moved with his parents and two sisters, Gail and Judy, to the small town of Sherman, Connecticut at age three. He spent his youth there before heading off to college in New Haven, Connecticut.

He currently (and for the foreseeable future) resides in the quiet town of Enfield, Connecticut, in a 1919 Colonial home with his wife Lyn and their dog Oscar.

He is the proud father of Laura and Nellie, and grandfather of Austin and Alex. Through his marriage to Lyn he is connected to her children Jimmy, Jackie, and Nicole, and grandchildren Ayana, Michaela, Jimmy, and Ronan.

This is his third book.

Printed in the USA
CPSIA information can be obtained
at www.ICGtesting.com
CBHW010839121123
1798CB00001B/2

9 798987 773918